MĀṆḌŪ

With the Kārikā of
GAUḌAPĀDA
and the Commentary of
ŚAṄKARĀCĀRYA

Translated by
Swāmi Gambhirānanda

Advaita Ashrama
(PUBLICATION DEPARTMENT)
5 DEHI ENTALLY ROAD • KOLKATA 700 014

Published by
Swami Bodhasarananda
Adhyaksha, Advaita Ashrama
Mayavati, Champawat, Uttarakhand
from its Publication Department, Kolkata
Email : mail@advaitaashrama.org
Website : www.advaitaashrama.org

First Edition, 1979
Fifth Impression, January 2010
1M1C

ISBN 978-81-7505-099-0

Printed in India at
Trio Process
Kolkata 700 014

PUBLISHER'S NOTE TO THE SECOND EDITION

It gives us pleasure to state that this second edition of the *Māṇḍūkya Upaniṣad* (with Gauḍapāda's *Kārikā*) has undergone a thorough revision by the translator himself.

Mayavati
1 January 1989

PUBLISHER

PUBLISHER'S NOTE TO THE FIRST EDITION

The *Māṇḍūkya Upaniṣad* and *Kārikā*, with the English translation of the commentary of Śrī Saṅkarācārya, is the third in the series to be published by us, after the *Aitareya Upaniṣad* and the *Muṇḍaka Upaniṣad*. This is to be followed very soon by the *Praśna Upaniṣad*. These four Upaniṣads together constitute Volume Two of *Eight Upaniṣads* by the same author.

In the translation of the commentary, the words quoted from the text by Śaṅkarācārya are given in italics. These are followed by commas and the English equivalents. Informative explanatory footnotes have been added wherever necessary.

This Upaniṣad derives its name after its seer Maṇḍūka, and belongs to the *Atharva-Veda*. Though it is the shortest of the principal Upaniṣads, having only twelve passages, it presents the quintessence of the entire Upaniṣadic teaching. It analyses the whole gamut of human consciousness, in the three states of waking (*jāgrat*), dream (*svapna*), and dreamless sleep (*suṣupti*). It asserts unequivocally that the ultimate Reality is non-dual (*advaita*) by adopting a unique method of investigating the three states of human consciousness, and proclaims the *mahāvākya* (sacred dictum): *ayamātmā brahma* (this self is Brahman).

This Upaniṣad provides a symbol for the meditation on, and the realization of, the supreme Reality; and that symbol is the mono-syllable *AUM*, the word of all words, comprising three sounds *A, U, M,* whose philosophical implications are elaborated in the text.

The language of this Upaniṣad is compact and concise. Hence the need of a *Kārikā* (expository treatise) by no less a person than Śrī Gauḍapāda, the *paramaguru* (spiritual teacher's teacher) of Śrī Śaṅkarācārya. The Ācārya considered it necessary to write a *bhāṣya* (commentary) on the *Kārikā* also, because of its lucid exposition of the text, apart from a commentary on the Upaniṣad proper. It can be said that the *Kārikā* is one of the earliest attempts to systematize the teachings of the Upaniṣads on rational lines. As such, it is looked upon as an authentic treatise on the Advaita Vedānta.

We earnestly hope that, with the publication of the present separate edition of this very important Upaniṣad, it will reach a wider circle of readers and arouse in them a genuine interest in the subject matter and help them to have correct idea of the Advaita Vedānta philosophy, which presents Truth without any consideration for creed, sect, colour, race, sex, or belief.

Mayavati — PUBLISHER

1 July 1979

CONTENTS

Key to Transliteration and Pronunciation ... x
List of Abbreviations xi
Chapter-I: Āgama-Prakaraṇa 3
Chapter-II: Vaitathya-Prakaraṇa 61
Chapter-III: Advaita-Prakaraṇa 98
Chapter-IV: Alātaśānti-Prakaraṇa 155
Index to the Text of Māṇḍūkya Upaniṣad 241
Index to the Ślokas of Gauḍapāda's Kārikā 242

KEY TO TRANSLITERATION AND PRONUNCIATION

		Sounds like			*Sounds like*
अ	a	o in s*o*n	ड	ḍ	d
आ	ā	a in m*a*ster	ढ	ḍh	dh in go*dh*ood
इ	i	i in *i*f	ण	ṇ	n in u*n*der
ई	ī	ee in f*ee*l	त	t	French t
उ	u	u in f*u*ll	थ	th	th in *th*umb
ऊ	ū	oo in b*oo*t	द	d	th in *th*en
ऋ	ṛ	somewhat between r and ri	ध	dh	theh in brea*the h*ere
ए	e	a in ev*a*de	न	n	n
ऐ	ai	y in m*y*	प	p	p
ओ	o	o in *o*ver	फ	ph	ph in loo*p-h*ole
औ	au	ow in n*ow*	ब	b	b
क	k	k	भ	bh	bh in a*bh*or
ख	kh	ckh in blo*ckh*ead	म	m	m
ग	g	g (hard)	य	y	y
घ	gh	gh in lo*g-h*ut	र	r	r
ङ	ṅ	ng	ल	l	l
च	c	ch (not k)	व	v	in a*v*ert
छ	ch	chh in cat*ch h*im	श	ś	sh
ज	j	j	ष	ṣ	sh in *sh*ow
झ	jh	dgeh in he*dgeh*og	स	s	s
ञ	ñ	n (somewhat)	ह	h	h
ट	ṭ	t		ṁ	m in hu*m*
ठ	ṭh	th in an*t-h*ill		ḥ	half h in hu*h*!

LIST OF ABBREVIATIONS

A.G.	...	Ānanda Giri
Ai.Ā.	...	Aitareya Āraṇyaka
Bṛ.	...	Bṛhadāraṇyaka Upaniṣad
Ch.	...	Chāndogya Upaniṣad
G.	...	Bhagavad Gītā
Īś.	...	Īśā Upaniṣad
Ka.	...	Kaṭha Upaniṣad
Ke.	...	Kena Upaniṣad
M.	...	Manu Saṁhitā
Mā.	...	Māṇḍūkya Upaniṣad
Mai.	...	Maitrāyaṇi Upaniṣad
Mbh.	...	Mahābhārata
Mu.	...	Muṇḍaka Upaniṣad
Nṛ.U.	...	Nṛsimha Uttaratāpani Upaniṣad
Pr.	...	Praśna Upaniṣad
Ṛ.	...	Ṛg-Veda
Śv.	...	Śvetāśvatara Upaniṣad
Tai.	...	Taittirīya Upaniṣad
Y.	...	Yajur-Veda

MĀṆḌŪKYA UPANIṢAD

ॐ भद्रं कर्णेभिः श्रृणुयाम देवा
भद्रं पश्येमाक्षभिर्यजत्राः ।
स्थिरैरङ्गैस्तुष्टुवाँसस्तनूभि-
र्व्यशेम देवहितं यदायुः ॥

स्वस्ति न इन्द्रो वृद्धश्रवाः
स्वस्ति नः पूषा विश्ववेदाः ।
स्वस्ति नस्ताक्ष्यो अरिष्टनेमिः
स्वस्ति नो बृहस्पतिर्दधातु ॥

ॐ शान्तिः शान्तिः शान्तिः ॥

Om! O gods, may we hear auspicious words with the ears; while engaged in sacrifices, may we see auspicious things with the eyes; while praising the gods with steady limbs, may we enjoy a life that is beneficial to the gods.

May Indra of ancient fame be auspicious to us; may the supremely rich (or all-knowing) Pūṣā (god of the earth) be propitious to us; may Garuḍa, the destroyer of evil, be well disposed towards us; may Bṛhaspati ensure our welfare.

Om! Peace! Peace! Peace!

MĀṆḌŪKYA UPANIṢAD

CHAPTER 1

ĀGAMA-PRAKARAṆA (ON THE VEDIC TEXT)

प्रज्ञानांशुप्रतानैः स्थिरचरनिकरव्यापिभिर्व्याप्य लोकान्
भुक्त्वा भोगान्स्थविष्ठान्पुनरपि धिषणोद्भासितान्कामजन्यान् ॥
पीत्वा सर्वान्विशेषान्स्वपिति मधुरभुङ्मायया भोजयन्नो
मायासंख्यातुरीयं परममृतमजं ब्रह्म यत्तन्नतोऽस्मि ॥१॥
यो विश्वात्मा विधिजविषयान्प्राश्य भोगान्स्थविष्ठान्
पश्चाच्चान्यान्स्वमतिविभवाञ्ज्योतिषा स्वेन सूक्ष्मान् ॥
सर्वानेतान्पुनरपि शनैः स्वात्मनि स्थापयित्वा
हित्वा सर्वान्विशेषान्विगतगुणगणः पात्वसौ नस्तुरीयः ॥२॥

Commentator's invocation: (1) I bow to that Brahman which after having enjoyed[1] (during the waking state) the gross objects by pervading all the human objectives through a diffusion of Its rays[2] of unchanging Consciousness that embraces all that moves or does not move; which again after having drunk[3] (during the dream state) all the variety of objects, produced by desire (as well as action and ignorance) and lighted up by the intellect,[4] sleeps while enjoying bliss and

[1] Enjoyment consisting in witnessing the various mental moods of happiness, sorrow, etc.

[2] The individual souls that are but reflections of Brahman on the intellect.

[3] I.e. having merged all in the unrealized Self.

[4] Existing only subjectively in the form of mental moods or impressions of past experience.

making us enjoy through Māyā; and which is counted as the Fourth[1] from the point of view of Māyā, and is supreme, immortal, and birthless.

(2) May that Fourth one protect us which, after having identified Itself with the universe,[2] enjoys (during the cosmic waking state) the gross objects created by virtue (and vice); which again (during the cosmic dream state[3]) experiences through Its own light the subtle objects of enjoyment that are called up by Its own intellect; which, further (in sound sleep or cosmic dissolution), withdraws promptly all these into Itself; and which lastly becomes free from all attributes by discarding every distinction and difference.

Introduction: 'The letter *Om* is all this. Of this a clear exposition (follows)' (Mā. 1). These four Chapters (of the *Kārikā*) that sum up the quintessence of the Vedāntic ideas are commenced with the text, 'The letter *Om* is all this,' etc. Accordingly, the connection, subject matter, and utility (of this treatise) need not be separately dealt with. The connection, subject matter, and utility that pertain to Vedānta itself should fit in here also.[4] Still they ought to be briefly stated by one who

[1] Not possessed of the three states of waking, dream, and sleep.

[2] The cosmic gross body of Virāṭ.

[3] As identified with the cosmic subtle body of Hiraṇyagarbha.

[4] The present book comprising the Upaniṣadic text and the *Kārikā* of Gauḍapāda forms a sort of a treatise on the Vedānta; and hence the four *anubandhas* or interconnecting elements — viz *adhikāri*, the person competent for study, *sambandha*, connection, e.g. that between the book and the subject matter, *viṣaya*, subject matter of the book, viz unity of the Self and Brahman, and *prayojana*, utility, viz liberation — are the same in both cases.

wants to explain a treatise. In this connection it is to be noted that by the very fact that a scripture (whether it be Vedānta or a treatise on it) reveals the spiritual disciplines conducive to the goal, it becomes endowed with a subject matter; and from this fact it becomes indirectly possessed of a distinct relationship, a subject matter, and utility.[1] What again is the objective in view? That is being explained: Just as the normal state of a man, afflicted by disease, consists in his getting cured of the disease, similarly the normalcy of the Self, stricken with identification with misery, is regained through the cessation of the phenomenal universe of duality. The end in view is the realization of non-duality. Since the phenomenal world of duality is a creation of ignorance, it can be eradicated through knowledge; and hence this book is begun in order to reveal the knowledge of Brahman. This fact is established by such Vedic texts as: 'Because when there is duality, as it were, then one smells something, one sees something,' and so on (Bṛ. II. iv. 14); 'When there is something else, as it were, then one can see something, one can know something' (Bṛ. IV. iii. 31); 'But when to the knower of Brahman everything has become the Self, then what should one see and through

[1] We are concerned primarily with knowledge and its result, and not with books. The result aimed at is liberation which follows from the realization of the non-difference of the Self and Brahman, and not from mere scriptures. Still the scriptures express that non-difference, and knowledge does not dawn without the help of scriptural deliberation. Thus, as the indirect means to knowledge, the scriptures become connected with the subject matter.

what? What should one know and through what?' (Bṛ. II. iv. 14).

That being so, the first chapter, devoted to a determination of the meaning of *Om*, is based on (Vedic) traditional knowledge and is an aid to the ascertainment of the reality of the Self. The second chapter is concerned with rationally proving the unreality of that phenomenal world of duality, on the cessation of which is attained non-duality, just as the reality of the rope is known on the elimination of the illusion of a snake etc. imagined on it. The third chapter is there to establish rationally the truth of non-duality, lest it, too, should be negated by a similar process of argument. The fourth chapter seeks to refute through their own arguments all the un-Vedic points of view which are antagonistic to the ascertainment of the truth of non-duality and which remain involved in this unreal duality by the very fact of their mutual antagonism.

How again does the ascertainment of the meaning of *Om* become an aid to the realization of the reality of the Self? The answer is: From such Vedic texts as, '(That goal which all the Vedas with one voice propound, which all the austerities speak of, and wishing for which people practise Brahmacarya)—it is this, viz *Om*' (Ka. I. ii. 15), 'This medium is the best' (Ka. I. ii. 17), 'O Satyakāma, this (*Om*) is verily Brahman, (superior and inferior)' (Pr. V. 2), 'Meditate on the Self as *Om*' (Mai. VI. 3), '*Om* is Brahman' (Tai. I. viii. 1), '*Om* indeed is all these' (Ch. II. xxiii. 3), it follows that just as the non-dual Self, notwithstanding the fact that It is the supreme Reality, can still be the substratum of all such illusions as the vital force, like the rope etc. becoming the substrata of the illusory snake etc., similarly it is but *Om* that appears as all the ramifications of speech which have for their contents such illusory manifestations of the Self as the vital force etc. And *Om* is essentially the same as the Self, since it denotes the latter. And all the illusory manifestations of the Self, such as the vital force etc., that are denoted by the modifications of *Om*, do not exist apart from their names, in accordance with the Vedic texts: 'All transformation has speech as its basis, and it is name only' (Ch. VI. i. 4), 'All this phenomenal creation of that Brahman is strung together by the thread of speech and by the strands of names', 'All these are but dependent on names'[1], and so on. Hence the Upaniṣad says, '*Om iti etat akṣaram idam sarvam*—the letter *Om* is all this.'

ओमित्येतदक्षरमिदꣳ सर्वं तस्योपव्याख्यानं भूतं भवद्भविष्यदिति सर्वमोङ्कार एव। यच्चान्यत् त्रिकालातीतं तदप्योङ्कार एव ॥१॥

1. This letter that is *Om* is all this. Of this a clear exposition (is started with): All that is past, present, or future is verily *Om*. And whatever is beyond the three periods of time is also verily *Om*.

As all these objects that are indicated by names are non-different from the names, and as names are non-different from *Om*, so *Om* is verily all this. And

[1] Names make empirical dealings possible for objects.

as the supreme Brahman is known through the relationship subsisting between name and its object, It, too, is but *Om*. *Tasya*, of that, of this letter, viz *Om*, that is the same as the supreme as well as the inferior Brahman; *upavyākhyānam*, a clear exposition, showing its proximity to Brahman by virtue of its being a means for the attainment of Brahman; the expression, 'is to be understood as started with', has to be supplied after 'clear exposition' to complete the sentence. *Bhūtam*, the past; *bhavat*, the present; *bhaviṣyat*, the future; *iti*, these, that is to say, whatever is circumscribed by the three periods of time; (*sarvam*) *oṅkāraḥ eva*, (all this) is but *Om*, in accordance with the reasons already advanced. *Ca yat trikālātītam*, and whatever else there is that is beyond the three periods of time, that is inferable from its effects but is not circumscribed by time, e.g. the Unmanifested and the rest; *tat api*, that, too; is *oṅkāraḥ eva*, verily *Om*.

Though a word and the thing signified are the same, still the presentation in the text, 'This letter that is *Om* is all this' etc. was made by giving greater prominence to the word. The very same thing that was presented through an emphasis on the word is being indicated over again with a stress on the thing signified, so that the unity of the name and the nameable may be comprehended. For otherwise, the nameable having been grasped as dependent on the name, the doubt may crop up that the identity of the nameable with the name is to be taken in a secondary sense. And the necessity of understanding their identity arises from the fact that (once this identity is established,) one can by a single effort eliminate both the name and the nameable to realize Brahman that is different from both. And this is what the Upaniṣad will say in, 'The quarters are the letters of *Om*, and the letters are the quarters' (8). The Upaniṣad adverts to the topic in, 'All this is surely Brahman' etc.

सर्वं ह्येतद् ब्रह्मायमात्मा ब्रह्म सोऽयमात्मा चतुष्पात् ॥२॥

2. All this is surely Brahman. This Self is Brahman. The Self, such as It is, is possessed of four quarters.

Sarvam etat, all this, all this that was spoken of as but *Om*; is *brahma*, Brahman. And that Brahman that was indirectly spoken of is being directly and specifically pointed out as, '*Ayam ātmā brahma*, this Self is Brahman.' In the text, 'This Self is Brahman', the very Self that will be presented as divided into four parts is being pointed out as one's innermost Self by the word '*ayam*, this', (accompanied) with a gesture of hand.[1] *Saḥ ayam ātmā*, that Self that is such, that is signified by *Om* and exists as the higher and lower Brahman; is *catuṣpāt*, possessed of four quarters, like a (*kārṣāpaṇa*) coin, but not like a cow.[2] As the Fourth (Turīya) is realized by successively merging the earlier three,

[1] By placing the hand on the heart.

[2] The word *pāda* may mean either foot or quarter. The second meaning applies here. A *kārṣāpaṇa* is divisible into sixteen smaller units. Four of these form a quarter. The smaller units lose their individuality in the bigger ones, as it were. So Viśva merges in Taijasa, Taijasa in Prājña, and Prājña in Turīya. The word 'quarter' is not used in any physical sense.

starting from Viśva, the word *pāda* (in the cases of Viśva, Taijasa and Prājña) is derived in the instrumental sense of that by which something is attained, whereas in the case of the Turīya the word *pāda* is derived in the objective sense of that which is achieved.

The Upaniṣad shows how the Self can be possessed of four quarters:

जागरितस्थानो बहिष्प्रज्ञः सप्ताङ्ग एकोनविंशतिमुखः स्थूलभुग्वैश्वानरः प्रथमः पादः ॥३॥

3. The first quarter is Vaiśvānara whose sphere (of action) is the waking state, whose consciousness relates to things external, who is possessed of seven limbs and nineteen mouths, and who enjoys gross things.

He (Vaiśvānara) who has the *jāgarita*, waking state, as His *sthāna*, sphere of activity, is *jāgaritasthānaḥ*. He who has His *prajñā*, awareness, *bahiḥ*, outside, directed to things other than Himself, is *bahiṣprajñaḥ*. The idea is that Consciousness appears as though related to outer objects, owing to ignorance. Similarly, He has seven limbs. For completing the imagery of Agnihotra sacrifice contained in, 'Heaven is verily the head of that Vaiśvānara-Self who is such; the sun is the eye, air is the vital force, space is the middle part, water is the bladder, and the earth indeed is the two feet' (Ch. V. xviii. 2), the Āhavanīya fire has been imagined as His mouth (ibid). He that is possessed of these seven limbs is *saptāṅgaḥ*. Similarly, He is *ekonaviṁśatimukhaḥ*, possessed of nineteen mouths — the (five) senses of perception and the (five) organs of action make up ten, the vital forces — Prāṇa and the rest — make up five, and (there are) mind (the thinking faculty), intellect, ego, and mind-stuff. These are mouths, since they are comparable to mouths; that is to say, they are the gates of experiences. Since through these aforesaid entrances Vaiśvānara, thus constituted, enjoys gross objects—viz sound and the rest—therefore He is *sthūlabhuk*, an enjoyer of the gross. He is called *vaiśvānaraḥ* because He leads in diverse ways all (*viśva*) beings (*nara*) (to their enjoyment). Or Vaiśvānara is the same as Viśvānara; He is called Vaiśvānara (all beings) since He encompasses all beings by virtue of His being non-different (in reality) from the Self (i.e. Virāṭ) comprising all the gross bodies. He is the *prathamaḥ pādaḥ*, the first quarter.[1] He gets this precedence, because the knowledge of the succeeding quarters is contingent on His knowledge.

Objection: The topic under discussion being the possession of four quarters by the indwelling Self referred to in the text, 'This Self is Brahman' etc., how is it that heaven and the rest are presented as the head etc.?

Answer: That is nothing incongruous, inasmuch as the intention is to show that the entire phenomenal universe and the world of gods, in the form of this (gross cosmic) Self, contribute to the constitution of the four parts.[2] If the presentation is made in this way, non-

[1] The first step to the knowledge of Brahman.

[2] The gross cosmic world, as constituting Virāṭ, is the first quarter. The subtle cosmic world, as constituting Hiraṇyagarbha,

duality stands established on the removal of the entire phenomenal world, and the Self existing in all beings is realized as one, and all beings are seen as existing in the Self.[1] And thus alone will stand affirmed the meaning of the Vedic text: He who sees all beings in the Self Itself, and the Self in all beings . . .' (Īś. 6). Otherwise, the indwelling Self, as circumscribed by one's own body, will alone be perceived, as It is by the Sāṁkhyas and others; and in that case the specific statement made by the Upaniṣads that It is non-dual (Mā. I. 7; Ch. VI. ii. 1) will remain unestablished for there will be no difference from the philosophies of the Sāṁkhyas and others. But as a matter of fact, it is desirable to find all the Upaniṣads propounding the unity of all the selves. Therefore it is but reasonable that, having in view the identity of this embodied Self (as Viśva) in the individual physical context with the Self as Virāṭ (i.e. Vaiśvānara) in the divine context, the former should be mentioned as possessed of seven limbs comprising such physical constituents as heaven etc. And this is confirmed by the logical grounds (for inferring unity) that is implied in, 'Your head would

---

is the second quarter. The cosmic world in its causal state (of ignorance) as constituting the Unmanifested, is the third quarter. That, again, when it is freed from all states of cause and effect and exists merely as the substratum of all, as Existence-Knowledge-Bliss, is the fourth quarter.

[1] Cf: सर्वभूतस्थमात्मानं सर्वभूतानि चात्मनि।
संपश्यन्नात्मयाजी वै स्वाराज्यमधिगच्छति ॥ (M. XII. 91)

have dropped off if you had not come to me'[1] (Ch. V. xii. 2).

This identity (of Viśva) with Virāṭ is suggestive of the unity (of Taijasa and Prājña) with Hiraṇyagarbha and the Unmanifested (respectively) as well. And this has been stated in the *Madhu-brāhmaṇa* (of the Bṛhadāraṇyaka Upaniṣad): '(The same with) the shining immortal being who is in this earth, and the (shining immortal) corporeal being (in the body). (These four are but this Self)' etc. (II. v. 1). As for the unity of the Self in sleep (Prājña) and the Unmanifested, it is a patent fact because of the absence of distinctions.[2] Such being the case, it will become proved that non-duality follows on the dissipation of all duality.

स्वप्नस्थानोऽन्तःप्रज्ञः सप्ताङ्ग एकोनविंशतिमुखः प्रविविक्तभुक्तैजसो द्वितीयः पादः ॥४॥

[1] Six Brāhmaṇas, who approached Aśvapati, used to worship particular limbs of Vaiśvānara as Vaiśvānara Himself. Aśvapati pointed out their mistakes and said that unless they had come to him for rectification, their head, eye, life, etc. would have been destroyed. But if the individual and Virāṭ are not the same, it is unreasonable to say, for instance, that from the mistaken worship of heaven (that is only the head of Virāṭ) as Virāṭ Himself, one's own head should drop off. The statement becomes reasonable only if the individual and Virāṭ are the same, so that the head of the one can be the head of the other.

[2] The individual sleeps by withdrawing all distinctions into himself, and in dissolution the Unmanifested, too, withdraws everything into itself. The 'Unmanifested' means here the 'inner Director' (Mā. 6) conditioned by Māyā, ruling from inside all.

4. Taijasa is the second quarter, whose sphere (of activity) is the dream state, whose consciousness is internal, who is possessed of seven limbs and nineteen mouths, and who enjoys subtle objects.

Taijasa that has the dream state as his sphere of activity is *svapnasthānaḥ*. The consciousness of the waking state, though it is only a state of mental vibration, is associated with many means, and it appears to be engrossed in external objects, and thus it leaves in the mind the corresponding impressions. Under the impulsion of ignorance, desire, and (past) action, that mind, thus possessed of the impressions like a piece of painted canvas, makes its appearance (in the dream state) just as in the waking state, but without any external means. In line with this is the statement, '(When he dreams), he takes away a little of (the impressions of) this all-embracing world (the waking state)' (Bṛ. IV. iii. 9). Similarly, in the Upaniṣad of the Atharva-Veda, after introducing (the subject) with '(All the senses) become one in the highest deity, the mind', it is said, 'In this dream state, this deity (the mind) experiences greatness' (Pr. IV. 5). The mind is *antaḥ*, internal in relation to the senses. And he whose *prajñā*, awareness in dream, takes the forms of the impressions in that (*antaḥ*, internal) mind, is *antaḥ-prajñaḥ*, aware of internal objects. He is called Taijasa (luminous), since he becomes the witness of the (modes of) cognition that is bereft of objects and appears only as a luminous thing. As Viśva is dependent on objects, he experiences the (modes of) gross cognition, whereas the awareness that is experienced here consists of mere impressions; and hence the enjoyment is subtle. The rest is common (with the earlier paragraph). Taijasa is the second quarter.

यत्र सुप्तो न कञ्चन कामं कामयते न कञ्चन स्वप्नं पश्यति तत् सुषुप्तम्। सुषुप्तस्थान एकीभूतः प्रज्ञानघन एवानन्दमयो ह्यानन्दभुक् चेतोमुखः प्राज्ञस्तृतीयः पादः ॥५॥

5. That state is deep sleep where the sleeper does not desire any enjoyable thing and does not see any dream. The third quarter is Prājña who has deep sleep as his sphere, in whom everything becomes undifferentiated, who is a mass of mere consciousness, who abounds in bliss, who is surely an enjoyer of bliss, and who is the doorway to the experience (of the dream and waking states).

Since sleep, consisting in the unawareness of Reality, is a common feature of the two states (of waking and dream) where there are the presence and absence (respectively, of perceptible gross objects), therefore the adverbial clause, 'Where the sleeper' etc.,[1] is used in order to keep in view the state of deep sleep. Or since sleep, consisting in the unawareness of Reality, is equally present in all the three states, deep sleep is being distinguished (by that clause) from the earlier

[1] That is to say, the portion 'does not desire any enjoyable thing' etc. occurring in the clause, 'Where the sleeper' etc.; for the portion 'does not' etc. distinguishes deep sleep from the other two states which have the common feature of unawareness.

two states.[1] *Yatra*, in which place, or at which time; *suptaḥ*, the sleeping man; *na paśyati*, does not see; *kañcana svapnam*, any dream; *na kāmayate*, does not desire; *kañcana kāmam*, any enjoyable thing—for in deep sleep there does not exist, as in the two earlier states, either dream, consisting in the perception of things otherwise than what they are, or any desire[2] —this is *tat suṣuptam*, that state of deep sleep. He who has got this state of deep sleep as his sphere is *suṣupta-sthānaḥ*. He is said to be *ekībhūtaḥ*, undifferentiated, since the whole host of duality, that are diversified as the two states (of waking and dream) and are but modifications of the mind, become non-discernible (in that state) without losing their aforesaid characteristics, just as the day together with the phenomenal world becomes non-discernible under the cover of nocturnal darkness. As such, conscious experiences, that are but vibrations of the mind in the waking and dream states, become solidified, as it were. This state is called *prajñānaghanaḥ*, a mass of consciousness, since it is characterized by the absence of discrimination. It is a mass of mere consciousness like everything ap-

[1] Since by the use of the portion, 'does not see any dream', that is to say, 'does not have any false perception of Reality', the other two states of dream and waking can be eliminated, the addition of the portion, 'does not desire any enjoyable thing', may seem to be redundant if we follow the first interpretation. To obviate this difficulty the second explanation is introduced. Non-perception of Reality being a common factor of the three states, deep sleep can be distinguished by the absence of desire.

[2] Thus either of the adverbial portions—viz absence of false perception, and freedom from desire — can be used for excluding the earlier two states.

pearing as a mass by becoming indistinguishable under nocturnal darkness. From the use of the word *eva*, merely, it follows that there is nothing of a separate class other than consciousness. And he is *ānandamayaḥ*, full of joy, his abundance of joy being caused by the absence of the misery involved in the effort of the mind vibrating as the objects and their experiencer; but he is not Bliss itself, since the joy is not absolute. Just as in common parlance, one remaining free from effort is said to be happy or *ānandabhuk*, an experiencer of joy, so this one, too, is called *ānandabhuk*, for by him is enjoyed this state that consists in extreme freedom from effort, in accordance with the Vedic text, 'this is its supreme bliss' (Bṛ. IV. iii. 32). He is *cetomukhaḥ*, since he is the doorway to the consciousness of the experiences in the dream and waking states. Or he is called *cetomukhaḥ*, because consciousness, appearing as empirical experience, is his doorway or entrance leading to the states of dream and waking. He is called *prājñaḥ*, Prājña, conscious *par excellence*, since in him alone is there the knowledge of the past and the future and of all things. Even though lying in deep sleep he is called Prājña (conscious) because of his having been so earlier (in the two former states of dream and waking); or he is called conscious, since he alone is possessed of the peculiar characteristics of mere (undiversified) consciousness, whereas the other two have diversified knowledge as well. This Prājña, as described, is the third quarter.

एष सर्वेश्वर एष सर्वज्ञ एषोऽन्तर्याम्येष योनिः सर्वस्य प्रभवाप्ययौ हि भूतानाम् ॥६॥

6. This one is the Lord of all; this one is Omniscient; this one is the inner Director (of all); this one is the Source of all; this one is verily the place of origin and dissolution of all beings.

Eṣaḥ, this one (this Prājña), when in his natural state; is surely *sarveśvaraḥ*, the Lord of all, of all diversity inclusive of the heavenly world; and contrary to what others believe in, He (the Lord of all) is not something intrinsically different from this one (that is Prājña), as is borne out by the Vedic text, 'O good-looking one, (the individual soul conditioned by) the mind is tethered to (that is to say, has for its goal) the Vital Force (which is Brahman)' (Ch. VI. viii. 2). This one, again, in his (state of) immanence in all diversity, is the knower of all; hence *eṣaḥ sarvajñaḥ*, this one is Omniscient. *Eṣaḥ*, this one, is; *antaryāmī*, the inner Controller; this one, indeed, becomes also the Director of all beings by entering inside (*antar*). For the same reason[1] he gives birth to the universe together with its diversities, as described before; and hence *eṣaḥ yoniḥ*, this one is the Source; *sarvasya*, of all. And since this is so, therefore this very one, is *hi*, certainly; *prabhava-apyayau*, the place of origin and dissolution; *bhūtānām*, of all beings.

GAUḌAPĀDA'S KĀRIKĀ

अत्रैतस्मिन् यथोक्तेऽर्थ एते श्लोका भवन्ति—

[1] Since Prājña is the Lord, Omniscient, and inner Director (in his identity with Brahman).

Pertaining to this aforesaid idea, here occur these verses:

Atra, with regard to the subject matter dealt with; *ete ślokāḥ bhavanti*, here occur these verses:

बहिष्प्रज्ञो विभुर्विश्वो ह्यन्तःप्रज्ञस्तु तैजसः।
घनप्रज्ञस्तथा प्राज्ञ एक एव त्रिधा स्मृतः ॥१॥

1. Viśva experiences the external things and is all-pervading; but Taijasa experiences the internal things; similarly, Prājña is a mass of consciousness. It is but the same entity that is thought of in three ways.

The purport of the verse is this: The transcendence of the three states by the Self, Its unity, purity, and unrelatedness (to anything) are proved by the fact of Its existence in the three states in succession and of Its being interlinked by memory as 'I'. This is borne out by the illustration of the great fish and others in the Vedic texts.[1]

दक्षिणाक्षिमुखे विश्वो मनस्यन्तस्तु तैजसः।
आकाशे च हृदि प्राज्ञस्त्रिधा देहे व्यवस्थितः ॥२॥

2. Viśva is met with in the right eye which is his

[1] 'As a great fish swims alternately to both the banks (of a river), eastern and western, so does this infinite being move to both these states — the dream and waking states' (Bṛ. IV. iii. 18). 'As a hawk or a falcon flying in the sky becomes tired, and stretching its wings is bound for its nest, so does this infinite being run for this state, where falling asleep he craves no desires and sees no dreams' (Bṛ. VI. iii. 19).

place of experience. But Taijasa is inside the mind. Prājña is in the space within the heart. In three ways he exists in the body.

This verse aims at discovering how all the three, starting with Viśva, are experienced in the waking state itself. Viśva, the witness of gross objects, is primarily experienced[1] in the *dakṣiṇa-akṣi*, right eye, that is his *mukha*, mouth (or place of experience); and this is in accordance with the Vedic text, 'This being who is in the right eye is named Indha' (Bṛ. IV. ii. 2). He who is Indha or Vaiśvānara, possessed of effulgence—the Virāṭ Self (identifying Itself with the cosmic gross body) that is within the sun—and he who is the (individual) Self (i.e. Viśva) in the (right) eye are identical.

Objection: Hiraṇyagarbha is different, and different also (is the soul that) is the knower of the body and senses, that exists in the right eye as the controller of the eyes, that is the cognizer, and that is the master of the body.

Answer: Not so, for in reality no difference is admitted, in accordance with the Vedic text, 'One effulgent being hidden in all creatures' (Śv. VI. 11), and the Smṛti texts, 'O scion of the Bharata dynasty, know me, again, as the knower of the bodies and senses, in all the bodies' (G. XIII. 2), 'Indivisible, and yet existing in all beings, as though divided' (G. XIII. 16).[2]

[1] By the adepts in meditation.

[2] Virāṭ is essentially identical with Hiraṇyagarbha, and so is the Prājña with them both.

Though Viśva exists equally in all the organs, he is specially referred to as existing in the right eye, for in the right eye is noticed the clarity of his (Viśva's) perception. The soul, with its abode in the right eye, perceives some form; and then closing the eyes and recollecting that very form sees it manifested, *manasi antaḥ*, inside the mind, in the form of impressions as in a dream.[1] As it is the case here, so is it in dream. Therefore, though Taijasa is within the mind, he is really the same as Viśva. On the cessation of the activity called memory, Prājña, sitting *ākāśe ca hṛdi*, in the space within the heart, becomes free from the diversity (of objects and their perceiving subject) and continues to be a mere mass of consciousness, for then there is no functioning of the mind.[2] Perception and recollection are merely vibrations of the mind; in the absence of these, there is mere existence in an unmanifested state, in the heart, in identification with the vital force, as is said in the Vedic text, 'It is the vital force indeed that engulfs all these' (Ch. IV. iii. 3). Taijasa is the same as Hiraṇyagarbha because of existing in the mind,[3] as is declared by the Vedic texts:

[1] This is how Taijasa is met with in the waking state. And Viśva and Taijasa are the same; for the same entity that sees as Viśva, recollects as Taijasa.

[2] This is how Prājña is met with in the waking state. When the mind ceases to act, the same entity assumes the characteristics of Prājña.

[3] Taijasa is conditioned by the individual mind, and Hiraṇyagarbha by the cosmic mind. But the individual and cosmic minds are the same; and so Taijasa and Hiraṇyagarbha, though conditioned by them, must be the same.

'(Being attached, he, together with the work, attains that result to which his) subtle body or mind (is attached)'[1] (Bṛ. IV. iv. 6), 'This Puruṣa identified with the mind,[2] (and resplendent, is realized within the heart)' (Bṛ. V. vi. 1), and so on.

Objection: The vital force is a manifested (i.e. perceptible) reality in deep sleep and the organs merge into it.[3] How can the vital force be unmanifested?

Answer: That is no defect; for an undifferentiated thing is characterized by absence of any distinction of time and space. Among those who think themselves to be intimately connected with the individualized vital force,[4] although the vital force appears to be differentiated so long as (individual) identification with Prāṇa persists still, since the self-identification with any speciality resulting from the delimitation of the body is absent in the vital force during deep sleep,

[1] Hiraṇyagarbha, as possessed of the power to act, is the soul within the subtle body (*liṅga*); and *liṅga* is equated with mind in the Vedic text. Therefore Taijasa and Hiraṇyagarbha are the same.

[2] Hiraṇyagarbha is but a special manifestation of the Puruṣa identified with the mind. And Taijasa's chief adjunct is the mind. Therefore they are the same.

[3] People sitting by a sleeping man clearly perceive the activities of the vital force (Prāṇa). And an additional argument proving that Prāṇa is a manifested entity is provided by the fact that the organs become identified with it in sleep. 'Unmanifested' means 'devoid of the limitations of time, space, and things'. Prāṇa is not so in deep sleep.

[4] They may think, 'This is my Prāṇa', 'That is his', and so on.

the vital force is then surely undifferentiated.[1] Just as in the case of people identifying themselves with individualized vital force, the vital force becomes unmanifested after death, similar, too, is the unmanifestedness in the state of absence of distinctions (in deep sleep) in the case of those who identify themselves with the vital force, and similar also is its potentiality to produce effects. And the witness in the state of unmanifestedness and deep sleep is the same (Consciousness).[2] Moreover, since the individuals who identify themselves with limitations, or witness those states, appear as identical with the Unmanifested, the foregoing attributes, 'in whom everything becomes undifferentiated', 'who is a mass of consciousness', etc., become appropriate with regard to him[3] (i.e. Prājña in deep sleep, identifying himself with Prāṇa). And there is also the reason adduced earlier[4].

Objection: Why should the Unmanifested be called Prāṇa (Vital Force)?

Answer: Because of the Vedic text, 'O good-looking one, (the individual soul conditioned by) the mind

1 Though to others it may appear to be manifested, to the sleeping man it is unmanifested, because for him the Prāṇa is then unassociated with any particular time or space.

2 Consciousness underlines the two entities conditioned by the unmanifested states on the divine and human planes.

3 Not only are the sleeper and the Unmanifested one from the standpoint of absence of distinction, but they are also one even when conditioned by limiting adjuncts.

4 The unity of the entity manifested on the divine and human planes.

is surely tethered to (that is to say, has for its goal) the Prāṇa' (Ch. VI. viii. 2).

Objection: In that text the word Prāṇa means Brahman that was introduced as Existence in the sentence, 'O good-looking one, in the beginning this was Existence alone' (Ch. VI. ii. 1).

Answer: That is no valid objection, for Existence was assumed there to be the seed (of creation). Though in that sentence the Existence-Brahman is denoted by the word Prāṇa, still that Existence(-Brahman) is called Prāṇa as well as Existence without ruling out Its being the source of the emergence of individual beings. Had the seedless (non-causal) state of Brahman been meant, the text would have declared, 'Not this, not this' (Bṛ. IV. iv. 22; IV. v. 15), 'From which speech turns back' (Tai. II. 9), 'That (Brahman) is surely different from the known, and, again, It is above the unknown' (Ke. I. 4), and so on, as it is also stated by the Smṛti, 'It is called neither existence nor non-existence' (G. XIII. 12). If Brahman in Its seedless (non-causal) state be meant there, then the individuals that merge in It in deep sleep and dissolution cannot reasonably re-emerge, and[1] there will be the possibility of the freed souls returning to take birth again, for in either case, the absence of cause is a common factor. Besides, in the absence of any seed (of the worldly state) to be burnt by the knowledge (of Brahman), knowledge itself becomes useless. Hence Exist-

[1] If anybody can re-emerge from sleep or dissolution, conceived of as nothing but identity with the pure Brahman, then. . .

ence is referred to as Prāṇa (in the Chāndogya Upaniṣad), and in all the Upaniṣads It is spoken of as the cause in all the Upaniṣads by assuming It (for the time being) to be the seed of others. And it is because of this that It is referred to—by refuting Its causal state—in such Vedic texts as, 'Superior to the (other) superior imperishable (Māyā) (Mu. II. i. 2), 'From which speech turns back' (Tai. II. 9), 'Not this, not this' (Bṛ. IV. iv. 22), etc. That supremely real state—free from causality, relation with body etc. and modes of waking etc.—of that very entity that is called Prājña, will be spoken separately in its aspect as the Turīya (Fourth). The causal state, too, is verily experienced in the body, inasmuch as an awakened man is seen to have such a recollection as, 'I did not know anything (in my deep sleep).' Hence it is said, '*Tridhā dehe vyavasthitaḥ*—existing in three ways in the body'.

विश्वो हि स्थूलभुङ्नित्यं तैजसः प्रविविक्तभुक् ।
आनन्दभुक्तथा प्राज्ञस्त्रिधा भोगं निबोधत ॥३॥

3. Viśva ever enjoys the gross; Taijasa enjoys the subtle; and similarly Prājña enjoys bliss. Know enjoyment to be threefold.

स्थूलं तर्पयते विश्वं प्रविविक्तं तु तैजसम् ।
आनन्दश्च तथा प्राज्ञं त्रिधा तृप्तिं निबोधत ॥४॥

4. The gross satisfies Viśva, and the subtle satisfies

Taijasa. And so also joy satisfies Prājña. Know enjoyment to be threefold.

The two verses need no explanation.

त्रिषु धामसु यद्भोज्यं भोक्ता यश्च प्रकीर्तितः।
वेदैतदुभयं यस्तु स भुञ्जानो न लिप्यते ॥५॥

5. He who knows both these—viz the enjoyment that there is in the three states, and that which is declared to be the enjoyer there—does not become affected even while enjoying.

Triṣu dhāmasu, in the three states, of waking and the rest; there is but one *bhojyam*, object of enjoyment, that appears in triple form, known as gross, subtle, and bliss. And the entity known by the names of Viśva, Taijasa, and Prājña, is *prakīrtitaḥ*, declared to be; the one *bhoktā*, enjoyer, because of their being unified together as one through the single concept of 'I am that', and because there is no distinction so far as cognition (by them) is concerned. He who *veda*, knows; *etat ubhayam*, both these, as diversified multifariously into enjoyers and the things of enjoyment; *saḥ*, he; *na lipyate*, does not become affected; *bhuñjānaḥ*, even while enjoying, because all that is enjoyable belongs to a single enjoyer. For nothing is added to or deducted from one's nature by one's own objects (of enjoyment or awareness)—as in the case of fire, which does not lose or gain (in its essential nature) by consuming its own fuel.

प्रभवः सर्वभावानां सतामिति विनिश्चयः।
सर्वं जनयति प्राणश्चेतोंशून् पुरुषः पृथक् ॥६॥

6. It is a well-established fact that origination belongs to all entities that have existence. Prāṇa creates all (objects); Puruṣa creates separately the rays of Consciousness (that are the living creatures).

Prabhavaḥ, origination, in their own respective apparent appearances consisting of names and forms created by ignorance; *sarvabhāvānām satām*, belongs to all the entities that exist[1] in their different modes of Viśva, Taijasa, and Prājña. It will be said later on, '... a barren woman's son is born neither through Māyā nor in reality' (*Kārikā*, III. 28). For, if birth really belongs to nonentities themselves, then Brahman, which is beyond all empirical relations, will be left without any ground of cognition,[2] and may be equated with nonentity. But as a matter of fact, it is seen that the snake and such other things created by

[1] Exist in their own substratum on which they are superimposed. In the sixth paragraph of the Upaniṣad, 'in this one is verily the place of origin', it was said that Prājña is the source of the phenomenal world. The question now is: 'Is he a producer of entities or nonentities?' The answer is that he produces entities which are a sort of reflection of Reality and are true so long as their substratum is kept in view.

[2] Logical ground of inference. If the effect is true, the cause can be inferred to be so; but if the effect is non-existing, the cause will be equally so. The inference with regard to Brahman will be like this: 'This world is produced from Existence (Brahman), for it is a superimposed thing like the snake on a rope.'

ignorance and sprouting from the seed of Māyā, and appearing as a rope etc., have their existence as the rope etc. (which are their substrata). For nobody perceives anywhere a rope-snake or a mirage if there is no substratum. Just as the snake surely had its existence as the rope before its illusory appearance as the snake, so also all positive entities, before their manifestation, certainly had their existence in the form of their cause, Prāṇa.[1] And it is therefore that the Upaniṣad, too, says, 'All this (that is in front) is but Brahman' (Mu. II. ii. 11), 'In the beginning this (universe) was but the Self' (Bṛ. I. iv. 1). *Prāṇaḥ janayati*, Prāṇa creates; *sarvam*, all. *Puruṣaḥ janayati*, Puruṣa creates; *pṛthak*, separately; *cetoṁśūn*, the rays of Consciousness, that issue out (from Puruṣa) like rays from the sun, that are the modes of the intelligence of Puruṣa who is by nature Consciousness, that are comparable to the reflections of the sun on water, and that appear divergently as Viśva, Taijasa, and Prājña in the different bodies of gods, animals, and others—(Puruṣa creates) all these rays of Consciousness that possess the characteristics of living creatures, that differ from what has assumed the appearance of objects, and that are similar (to Puruṣa) just as the sparks of fire (are to fire), or the reflections of the sun on water (are to the sun). But Prāṇa, or the Self in the causal state, creates all other entities[2] as shown in the Vedic texts: 'As a spider (spreads and withdraws

[1] Prāṇa is Brahman considered as an unknown entity but identified with Existence and serving as the source of all.

[2] Existing in the form of objects, as opposed to the subjects.

its thread)' (Mu. I. i. 7), and 'as from fire tiny sparks fly in all directions' (Bṛ. II. i. 20).

विभूतिं प्रसवं त्वन्ये मन्यन्ते सृष्टिचिन्तकाः ।
स्वप्नमायासरूपेति सृष्टिरन्यैर्विकल्पिता ॥७॥

7. Others steeped in cognition about creation consider origination as an exuberance (of God), while by others it is imagined that creation is comparable to dream or magic.

Sṛiṣṭicintakāḥ, people steeped in the thought (or theories) of creation; *manyante*, consider; that creation is a *vibhūti*, exuberance, (a demonstration of the superhuman power), of God. The idea implied is that for people who think of the supreme Reality there is no interest in questions regarding creation, (which is illusory) as is declared in the Vedic text, 'Indra (the Lord), on account of Māyā, is perceived as manifold' (Bṛ. II. v. 19). For those who observe a magician throw up a rope into the sky, ascend it bearing arms and vanish out of sight, and engage in a fight in which he is cut to pieces and falls to rise up again, do not evince any interest in deliberating on the reality of the magic and its effect conjured up by him. So also, analogous to the spreading out of the rope by the magician, is this manifestation of deep sleep, dream, and so on; comparable to the magician who has climbed up the rope are the Prājña, Taijasa, and the rest in those states; and different from the rope and the man who has climbed up it is the real magician. Just as that very magician stands on the ground, invisible because of his magical cover, similar is the supreme Reality called Turīya. Therefore the noble people, aspiring to liberation, evince interest in the contemplation of that Turīya alone, but not so in that of creation which serves no purpose. Hence these theories are advanced only by those who cogitate about creation. This fact is stated in *svapnamāyāsarūpā*, of the same nature as dream and magic.[1]

इच्छामात्रं प्रभोः सृष्टिरिति सृष्टौ विनिश्चिताः ।
कालात्प्रसूतिं भूतानां मन्यन्ते कालचिन्तकाः ॥८॥

8. With regard to creation some have the firm conviction that creation is a mere will of the Lord. People engrossed in the thought of time (to wit, astrologers) consider that birth of beings is from time.

Sṛṣṭiḥ, creation; is *icchāmātram*, a mere will; *prabhoḥ*, of the Lord, because His will is unfailing. A pot, for instance, is a mere thought (of the potter), and it is nothing beyond thought. Some think that creation is from time alone.

भोगार्थं सृष्टिरित्यन्ये क्रीडार्थमिति चापरे ।
देवस्यैष स्वभावोऽयमाप्तकामस्य का स्पृहा ॥९॥

9. Some others say that creation is for the enjoy-

[1] This differs from the Vedāntic position in believing that dream is true so far as it reflects the phenomenal realities of the waking state, and that the incantations etc., conjuring up magical illusions, are themselves empirically true, though the magical objects are false.

ment (of God), while still others say that it is for (His) disport. But it is the very nature of the Effulgent Being, (for) what desire can One have whose desire is ever fulfilled?

Others think that *sṛṣṭiḥ*, creation; is *bhogārtham*, for the sake of enjoyment; (and) *krīḍārtham*, for the sake of disport. These two views are refuted by '*devasya eṣaḥ svabhāvaḥ ayam*, of the Effulgent Being this is the nature'[1] etc., by basing the argument on the Nature (of God). Or, all the points of view[2] are refuted by asserting, '*Āptakāmasya kā spṛhā*, what desire can One have whose desire is ever fulfilled?' For apart from the fact that the rope etc. are constituted by natural ignorance,[3] no cause can be ascertained for their appearing as snake etc.

UPANIṢAD

The fourth quarter which follows in order has to be stated; hence this is presented (by the Upaniṣad) in '*nāntaḥ-prajñam*, not conscious of internal world' etc. Since It (i.e. Turīya) is devoid of every characteristic that can make the use of words possible, It is not describable through words; and hence the (Upaniṣad)

[1] Nature, otherwise known as Māyā, is without any beginning though it is directly perceived. This being so, no motive for creation should be sought.

[2] Presented in the verses 7 and 8, and the first line of verse 9.

[3] Ignorance about the rope etc. that are the substrata of the illusory things like snake etc.

seeks to indicate Turīya merely through the negation of attributes.

Objection: In that case is It a mere void?

Answer: No, for an unreal illusion cannot exist without a substratum; for the illusion of silver, snake, human being, mirage, etc., cannot be imagined to exist apart from the (corresponding) substrata of the mother of pearl, rope, stump of a tree, desert, etc.[1]

Objection: In that case, just as a pot etc. that hold water etc. are denoted by words, so also Turīya should be specified by (positive) words, and not by negations, for It is the substratum of all such illusion as Prāṇa etc.

Answer: Not so, because the illusion of Prāṇa and the rest is unreal just as silver and the rest are on the mother of pearl etc. For a relation between the real and the unreal does not lend itself to verbal representation, since the relation itself is unsubstantial. Unlike a cow, for instance, the Self, in Its own reality, is not an object of any other means of knowledge; for the Self is free from all adventitious attributes. Nor like a cow etc. does It belong to any class; because, by virtue of Its being one without a second, It is free from generic and specific attributes. Nor is It possessed of activity like a cook for instance, since It is devoid of all action. Nor is It possessed of qualities like blueness etc., It being free from qualities. Therefore It baffles all verbal description.

[1] Since an illusion is perceived as soaked in the idea of existence, it cannot have non-existence as its basis.

Objection: It will, in that case, serve no useful purpose, like the horn of a hare and such other things.

Answer: Not so; for when Turīya is realized as the Self, it leads to the cessation of craving for the non-Self, just as the hankering for silver ceases on recognizing the nacre. Indeed, there can be no possibility of such defects as ignorance, desire, and the like, after the realization of Turīya as one's Self. Nor is there any reason why Turīya should not be realized as identical with one's Self, inasmuch as all the Upaniṣads aim at this conclusion, as is evidenced by the texts, 'Thou art That' (Ch. VI. viii-xvi), 'This Self is Brahman' (Bṛ. II. v. 19), 'That which is the Self is Truth' (Ch. VI. viii.7), 'The Brahman that is immediate and direct' (Bṛ. III. iv. 1), 'Since He is coextensive with all that is external and internal and since He is birthless . . .' (Mu. II. i. 2), 'The Self indeed is all this' (Ch. VII. xxv. 2), and so on.

This very Self, that is the supreme Reality but has false appearances, has been spoken of as possessed of four quarters. Its unreal form has been dealt with, which is a creation of ignorance and which is analogous to a snake superimposed on a rope, and consists of the three quarters that are related (mutually) like the seed and its sprout.[1] Now, in the text beginning with, '*nāntaḥprajñam*, not conscious of the internal world', the Upaniṣad speaks of the non-causal, supremely real state, comparable to a rope etc., by way of eliminating the aforesaid three states, com-

[1] By way of cause and effect.

parable to the snake etc. (superimposed on the rope etc.).

नान्तःप्रज्ञं न बहिष्प्रज्ञं नोभयतःप्रज्ञं न प्रज्ञानघनं न प्रज्ञं नाप्रज्ञम् । अदृष्टमव्यवहार्यमग्राह्यमलक्षणमचिन्त्यमव्यपदेश्यमेकात्मप्रत्ययसारं प्रपञ्चोपशमं शान्तं शिवमद्वैतं चतुर्थं मन्यन्ते स आत्मा स विज्ञेयः ॥७॥

7. They consider the Fourth to be that which is not conscious of the internal world, nor conscious of the external world, nor conscious of both the worlds, nor a mass of consciousness, nor conscious, nor unconscious; which is unseen, beyond empirical dealings, beyond the grasp (of the organs of action), uninferable, unthinkable, indescribable; whose valid proof consists in the single belief in the Self; in which all phenomena cease; and which is unchanging, auspicious, and non-dual. That is the Self, and That is to be known.

Objection: The start was made with the premise that the Self is possessed of four quarters. Then, after the presentation of the three quarters, it has become evident that the fourth is different from those three that are conscious of the internal world, and so on; and hence the negation through 'not conscious of the internal world' etc. becomes futile.

Answer: Not so; for as the true nature of the rope is realized through the negation of the illusions of a snake etc., so the very Self, subsisting usually in the three states, is sought to be established as Turīya in the same way as is done in the case of the text, 'That thou art'[1] (Ch. VI. viii). For if Turīya, whose characteristics are dissimilar to those of the Self in the three states, be really different (from the Self), then owing to the absence of any means for realizing Turīya the scriptural instruction would be useless or Turīya will be reduced to a non-entity. On the view, however, that like the rope, imagined variously as a snake etc., the Self, too, though one, is imagined in the three states to be possessed of such attributes as consciousness of the internal world etc., there follows in the Self the cessation of the phenomenal world of misery simultaneously with the valid knowledge arising from the negation of such attributes as being conscious of he internal world; and therefore there remains no need to search for any other means of knowledge or any other discipline (like constant thinking) for the realization of Turīya. This is similar to what happens in the case of the knowledge of the rope where the elimination of the snake from the rope occurs simultaneously with the discrimination between the rope and the snake.[2] On the contrary, by those who hold the view that in the act of knowing a pot, for instance,

[1] This positive statement is interpreted not literally, but figuratively to mean that 'Thou', which is the individual soul, is identical with 'That', which is God, when both are bereft of conditioning factors.

[2] Since along with the discriminating knowledge in the form, 'This is a rope and not a snake', the cessation of the snake comes simultaneously, one need not search for a separate result to issue out of the direct perception of the rope, or for any other means of its knowledge, or any other aid to it.

an instrument of knowledge engages in some other activity in addition to the removal of darkness (from the pot etc.), it may as well be held that in the matter of splitting wood, the act of splitting engages in doing something to one of the two parts in addition to removing the adhesion of the two members.[1] On the other hand, if it is true that the means of knowledge, engaged in distinguishing a jar from the darkness (covering it), fulfils its goal by merely removing the unwanted darkness, just as the act of cutting, aimed at tearing apart the adhesion of the parts of the wood to be split, fully serves its purpose by separating the parts, then the knowledge of the jar emerges immediately; and it is not achieved by any instrument of knowledge. Just as it is here, so in the case of Turīya the instrument of knowledge—which is nothing but a valid knowledge arising from negation and intended to separate such ideas as being 'conscious of the internal world' that are superimposed on the Self—has no other action on Turīya, apart from eliminating the unwanted attributes like being 'conscious

[1] The *objection* was: 'The result of applying an instrument of knowledge to any object is the revelation of the object and not the mere removal of any illusion created by darkness or "ignorance".' The *answer* is: 'An instrument of knowledge fulfils its purpose by removing the darkness of ignorance from its object. The revelation comes *pari passu*, as a matter of course. If the instrument of knowledge is supposed to serve the additional purpose of adding a fresh feature, like revelation, to its object, then one may as well argue that the cutting of wood aims not only at removing the adhesion of the two parts, but also at adding something to either of the two parts.'

of the internal world';[1] for simultaneously with the cessation of such attributes as being 'conscious of the internal world', there comes about the eradication of such distinctions as the knower, (the known, and the knowledge). So also it will be said, 'Duality ceases to exist after realization' (*Kārikā*, I. 18), for knowledge (as a mental state) does not continue for a second moment following that of the cessation of duality. Should it, however, continue, it will lead to infinite regress resulting in non-cessation of duality.[2] Therefore the conclusion arrived at is that all evils, such as being 'conscious of the internal world', superimposed on the Self, cease simultaneously with the application (i.e. birth) of the instrument (of illumination) which is nothing but a valid knowledge arising from negation (of duality).

By the phrase, '*nāntaḥ-prajñam*, not conscious of the internal world', is eliminated Taijasa. By '*na bahiṣ-prajñam*, not conscious of the outside world', is eliminated Viśva. By '*na ubhayataḥ-prajñam*, not conscious of either' is ruled out the intermediate state between dream and waking. By '*na prajñānaghanam*, not a mass of consciousness' is denied the state of deep sleep, for this consists in a state of latency where every-

[1] Turīya is self-effulgent and does not require to be illumined by any instrument of knowledge.

[2] If the knowledge calculated to eliminate duality persists after serving its purpose, some other knowledge will be needed to eliminate it. That other knowledge will again require a third for a similar purpose, and so on. To avoid this contingency, the final knowledge must be assumed to be self-immolating.

thing becomes indistinguishable. By '*na prajñam*, nor conscious' is denied being aware of all objects simultaneously (by a single act of consciousness). By '*na aprajñam*, nor unconscious' is negated insentience.

Objection: Since attributes like being 'conscious of the internal world' are perceived as inhering in the Self, how, again, can they be understood to become non-existent, like the snake etc. in the rope etc., by a mere negation?

The *answer* is: Since like the imaginary diversities —such as a snake, a line of water, etc., superimposed on the rope—the above states (appearing on the Self) mutually rule out each other, though they are in essence one with the witnessing Consciousness, and since the witnessing Consciousness in Its essence is unchanging in all the states, it follows that the witness is true.

Objection: It changes (i.e. disappears) in deep sleep.

Answer: Not so, for one in deep sleep is cognized (as soaked in Consciousness);[1] and this is borne out by the Vedic text, 'for the knower's function of knowing can never be lost' (Bṛ. IV. iii. 30).

Hence, It is *adṛṣṭam*, unseen.[2] Since It is unseen (i.e. unperceived), therefore It is *avyavahāryam*, beyond

[1] One rising from deep sleep says, 'I slept soundly, and I was not aware of anything'. This memory would not have been possible unless the state was witnessed with the help of Consciousness so as to produce the necessary impressions.

[2] Not the object of any sense of knowledge.

empirical dealings; *agrāhyam*, beyond the grasp, of the organs of action; *alakṣaṇam*, without any logical ground of inference, that is to say, uninferable. Therefore It is *acintyam*, unthinkable. Hence It is *avyapadeśyam*, indescribable, by words. It is *eka-ātma-pratyaya-sāram*, to be spotted by the unchanging belief that It is the same Self that subsists in the states of waking and so on. Or, the Turīya that has for Its *sāra*, valid proof, *eka ātmapratyaya*, the single belief in the Self, is the *eka-ātmapratyaya-sāra*. And this is in accord with the Vedic text: 'The Self alone is to be meditated upon' (Bṛ. I. iv. 7).

The attributes, such as being 'conscious of the internal world', belonging to the possessors of the states (viz Viśva, Taijasa, and Prājña), have been negated. In '*prapañcopaśamam*, the one in whom all phenomena have ceased', etc. are being denied the attributes of the states of waking etc. Hence It is *śāntam*, unchanging;[1] *śivam*, auspicious.[2] Since It is *advaitam*, non-dual, free from illusory ideas of difference; therefore *manyante*, (they) consider It to be; the Turīya, *caturtham*, the Fourth, being distinct from the three quarters that are mere appearances. '*Saḥ ātmā*, That is the Self; *saḥ vijñeyaḥ*, That is to be known'—this is said to imply that just as the rope is known to be different from the snake, the crack on the ground, or the stick, superimposed on it, similarly, that Self is to be known (as different from the superimposed states)—the Self that is presented in the sentence 'That thou art' (Ch.

[1] Free from love, hatred, etc.

[2] Absolutely pure; supreme Bliss and Consciousness in essence.

VI. viii-xvi), and that has been spoken of by such texts as 'He is never seen, but is the witness' (Bṛ. III. vii. 23), 'for the vision of the witness can never be lost' (Bṛ. IV. iii. 23), etc. 'That is to be known'—this is spoken of from the standpoint of the previous state of ignorance,[1] for on the dawn of knowledge, no duality is left.

GAUḌAPĀDA'S KĀRIKĀ

Here occur these verses (of Gauḍapāda):

निवृत्तेः सर्वदुःखानामीशानः प्रभुरव्ययः ।
अद्वैतः सर्वभावानां देवस्तुर्यो विभुः स्मृतः ॥१०॥

10. The unchanging non-dual One is the ordainer —the Lord—in the matter of eradicating all sorrows. The effulgent Turīya is held to be the all-pervasive source of all objects.

Nivṛtteḥ, in the matter of eradication; *sarvaduḥkhā-nām*, of all sorrows, represented by Viśva, Taijasa, and Prājña; the Self that is Turīya is *īśānaḥ*, the ordainer. '*Prabhuḥ*, Lord' is an explanation of the word *īśānaḥ*. The idea is that He is the Lord capable of ordaining the cessation of sorrow; for sorrow ceases as a result of His knowledge. (He is) *avyayaḥ*, un-

[1] The Self, defying all description, cannot be known objectively. But since in the state of ignorance one understands knowledge as having objective reference, the text follows that trend of thought here as well.

changing, that is to say, does not deviate from His nature. Why is this so? Because He is *advaitaḥ*, non-dual, on account of the falsity of all objects, like the snake on a rope. He who is this *devaḥ*, effulgent One, so called because of His self-effulgence; *smṛtaḥ*, held to be; *turīyaḥ*, the Fourth; and *vibhuḥ*, the Omnipresent (source)[1].

For determining the true nature of Turīya, the generic and specific characteristics of Viśva and the rest are being ascertained:

कार्यकारणबद्धौ ताविष्येते विश्वतैजसौ ।
प्राज्ञः कारणबद्धस्तु द्वौ तौ तुर्ये न सिध्यतः ॥११॥

11. Those two, viz Viśva and Taijasa, are held to be conditioned by cause and effect. Prājña is conditioned by cause. But both these do not exist in Turīya.

Kārya, derived in the sense of anything produced, means the state of being the effect. *Kāraṇa*, derived in the sense of anything that acts, means the causal state. Those two, viz *viśva-taijasau*, Viśva and Taijasa, as described earlier; *iṣyete*, are held to be; (*kārya-kāraṇa-baddhau*), bound by, conditioned by, the states of seed and fruit, consisting in the non-apprehension and misapprehension of Reality. But Prājña is bound by the causal state alone. The non-apprehension of

[1] Turīya is *vibku*, because the three different (*vividha*) states issue (*bhavanti*) from Him — A.G.

Reality alone is the cause of bringing about the state of Prājña. Therefore *tau dvau*, both these two—the causal and the resultant conditions, the non-apprehension and misapprehension of Reality, respectively—*na sidhyataḥ turye*, do not exist, that is to say, are not possible, in Turīya.

नात्मानं न परांश्चैव न सत्यं नापि चानृतम्।
प्राज्ञः किञ्चन संवेत्ति तुर्यं तत् सर्वदृक् सदा ॥१२॥

12. Prājña does not comprehend anything—neither himself nor others, neither truth nor falsehood. But that Turīya is for ever everything and the witness.

How, again, is Prājña conditioned by the causal state, and how are the bondages of non-apprehension and misapprehension impossible in the case of Turīya? Since unlike Viśva and Taijasa, Prājña *na saṁvetti*, does not apprehend; *kiñcana*, anything, any external duality that is different from the Self and is born of the seed of ignorance, therefore he is conditioned by the darkness of non-perception of Reality, which is the seed of false perception. Since *tat*, that; Turīya is *sadā*, for ever; *sarva-dṛk*, all (*sarva*) that there is as well as its witness (*dṛk*), there being nothing besides Turīya; therefore the seed consisting in non-perception of Reality does not exist there (in the Turīya). And just because of this there is also the absence in Turīya of false perception resulting from non-perception; for in the sun, which is ever resplendent, there is no possibility of the opposite, darkness, or shining in any way other than that of the sun— in conformity with the Vedic text, 'for the vision of the witness can never be lost' (Bṛ. IV. iii. 23). Or, Turīya is said to be the '*sarva-dṛk*, seer of everything' for ever, because it is but Turīya who, by existing in all beings during the dream and the waking states, seems to be the seer of everything. For the Upaniṣad says, 'There is no other witness but This' (Bṛ.III. viii. 11).

द्वैतस्याग्रहणं तुल्यमुभयोः प्राज्ञतुर्ययोः।
बीजनिद्रायुतः प्राज्ञः सा च तुर्ये न विद्यते ॥१३॥

13. Non-perception of duality is common to both Prājña and Turīya. Prājña is endued with sleep that is a causal state. But in Turīya that sleep does not exist.

This verse is meant to remove the doubt arising from another source. 'The non-perception of duality being similar, why should Prājña alone be conditioned by causality and not Turīya?'—this doubt that may arise is being refuted. The reason is that Prājña is *bīja-nidrā-yutaḥ*; *nidrā*, sleep, consists in the non-perception of Reality, and that itself is the *bīja*, seed of the birth of the cognition of varieties; and Prājña is *yutaḥ*, endued by this *bījanidrā*, sleep that is a causal state. That sleep, consisting in the non-perception of Reality, *na vidyate*, does not exist; *turye*, in Turīya, because of His being by nature a constant witness. Therefore in Him there is no bondage of the causal state. This is the purport.

स्वप्ननिद्रायुतावाद्यौ प्राज्ञस्त्वस्वप्ननिद्रया ।
न निद्रां नैव च स्वप्नं तुर्ये पश्यन्ति निश्चिताः ॥१४॥

14. The earlier two are endued with dream and sleep, but Prājña is endued with dreamless sleep. People of firm conviction do not see either sleep or dream in Turīya.

Svapna, dream, consists in false perception, like that of a snake on a rope. *Nidrā*, sleep, has been spoken of as darkness, consisting in non-perception of Reality. By these two—dream and sleep—are endued Viśva and Taijasa; and this is why they have been referred to as conditioned by the states of cause and effect (*Kārikā*, I. 11); whereas Prājña is conditioned by sleep alone, unassociated with dream; and hence he has been referred to as conditioned by the causal state. *Niścitāḥ*, those with firm conviction, the knowers of Brahman; *na paśyanti*, do not see, both these in Turīya, these being of an opposite nature, like darkness with regard to the sun. Therefore it has been said that Turīya is not conditioned by the states of cause and effect.

It is being shown when one becomes firmly rooted in Turīya:

अन्यथा गृह्णतः स्वप्नो निद्रा तत्त्वमजानतः ।
विपर्यासे तयोः क्षीणे तुरीयं पदमश्नुते ॥१५॥

15. Dream belongs to one who sees falsely, and sleep to one who does not know Reality. When the two

errors of these two[1] are removed, one attains the state that is Turīya.

Svapnaḥ, dream; comes to one *gṛhṇataḥ*, who cognizes Reality; *anyathā*, falsely, like the cognition of a snake on a rope, in the states of dream and waking. *Nidrā*, sleep—belonging to one *ajānataḥ tattvam*, not cognizing Reality—is equally present in all the three states. Dream and sleep being the common features of both Viśva and Taijasa, they are treated as one. Since in these two states sleep is of secondary importance owing to the predominance of false perception, the error (in these states) is equated with dream. But in the third state the error takes the form of sleep alone, consisting in non-perception of Reality. Therefore when *tayoḥ*, of these two (Viśva-Taijasa and Prājña), existing in the states of effect and cause; *viparyāse*, the two errors, consisting in false perception and non-perception, and constituting the two bondages in the form of effect and cause; *kṣīṇe*, are eradicated on the cognition of the supreme Reality; then one *aśnute*, attains; *turīyam padam*, the state of Turīya. The idea is that, as he does not perceive both kinds of bondages there, he becomes firmly rooted in Turīya.

अनादिमायया सुप्तो यदा जीवः प्रबुध्यते ।
अजमनिद्रमस्वप्नमद्वैतं बुध्यते तदा ॥१६॥

16. When the individual, sleeping under the in-

[1] Viśva and Taijasa constitute one factor and Prājña the other. This is why '*tayoḥ*, of these two' is used in the dual number.

fluence of beginningless Māyā, is awakened, then he realizes the birthless, sleepless, dreamless, non-dual (Turīya).

This one, the *jīvaḥ*, the transmigrating individual soul; that is *suptaḥ*, asleep; while seeing in both the (waking and dream) states such dreams as 'This is my father', 'This is my son', 'This is my grandson', 'This is my field', 'These are my animals', 'I am their master', 'I am happy, miserable', 'I am despoiled by this one, and I have gained through this one', and so on, under the influence of dream that is but Māyā whose activity has no beginning and which has the two facets of non-perception of Reality or the causal state, and false perception of Reality. *Yadā*, when by a most gracious teacher, who has realized the Truth that forms the purport of the Upaniṣads, he (the individual) is awakened through the teaching, 'Thou art not a bundle of causes and effects, but "Thou art That"', then that individual understands thus. How? (Thus): (He knows the) *ajam*, birthless, which is called so since in It there is no external or internal mutation, starting with birth, that positive objects are heir to; the idea is that It is externally and internally devoid of all mutations that phenomenal objects are subject to. (He knows the) *anidram*, sleepless (Turīya), since in It there is no sleep or the causal state, consisting in the darkness of ignorance that is the cause of birth and so on. Since that Turīya is sleepless, therefore (he realizes) It is *asvapnam*, dreamless, false perception (*svapna*) being based on non-perception (*nidrā*). Since It is sleepless and dreamless, therefore the individual, *tadā*, then; *budhyate*, realizes the birthless, non-dual Turīya as his Self.

प्रपञ्चो यदि विद्येत निवर्तेत न संशयः ।
मायामात्रमिदं द्वैतमद्वैतं परमार्थतः ॥१७॥

17. It is beyond question that the phenomenal world would cease to be if it had any existence. All this duality that is nothing but Māyā, is but non-duality in reality.

If one is to be awakened by negating the phenomenal world, how can there be non-duality so long as the phenomenal world persists? The answer is: Such indeed would be the case *yadi prapañcaḥ vidyeta*, if the phenomenal world had existence. But being superimposed like a snake on a rope, it does not exist. *Na saṁśayaḥ*, there is no doubt; that if it had existed, *nivarteta*, it would cease to be. Certainly, it is not that the snake, fancied on the rope through an error of observation, exists there in reality and is then removed by correct observation. Verily, it is not that the magic conjured up by a magician exists in reality and is then removed on the removal of the optical illusion of its witness. Similarly, *māyāmātram idam dvaitam*, this duality that is nothing but Māyā, and is called the phenomenal world; is *paramārthataḥ*, in supreme Truth; *advaitam*, non-dual, just like the rope and the magician. Therefore the purport is that there is no such thing as the world which appears or disappears.

विकल्पो विनिवर्तेत कल्पितो यदि केनचित् ।
उपदेशादयं वादो ज्ञाते द्वैतं न विद्यते ॥१८॥

18. Diversity would disappear if it had been imagined by anyone. This kind of talk is for the sake of (making) instruction (possible). Duality ceases to exist after realization.

How can such fancies as instruction, instructor, and the instructed disappear? To this the answer is: *Vikalpaḥ*, diversity; *vinivarteta*, would discontinue; *yadi*, if; it had been *kalpitaḥ*, imagined; *kenacit*, by anybody. Just as this phenomenal world is analogous to magic or a snake superimposed on a rope, so also such fancies as the differences of the instructed and so on are there only before enlightenment, *upadeśāt*, for the sake of instruction; hence *ayam vādaḥ*, this talk—of instructor, instruction, and instructed—is for the sake of instruction. When the effect of instruction is accomplished, *jñāte*, on the realization of the supreme Reality; *dvaitam na vidyate*, duality ceases to exist.

UPANIṢAD

सोऽयमात्माऽध्यक्षरमोङ्कारोऽधिमात्रं पादा मात्रा मात्राश्च पादा अकार उकारो मकार इति ॥८॥

8. That very Self, considered from the standpoint of the syllable (denoting It) is *Om*. Considered from the standpoint of the letters (constituting *Om*), the quarters (of the Self) are the letters (of *Om*), and the letters are the quarters. (The letters are): *a*, *u*, and *m*.

Saḥ ayam ātmā, that very Self, which was equated with *Om* in, 'This Self is possessed of four quarters'

(Mā. 2), by giving predominance to the object denoted (by *Om*)—that very Self; *adhyakṣaram*, from the standpoint of the syllable, (is *Om*) when explained with emphasis on the syllable. Which again is that syllable? That is being stated: *Oṅkāraḥ*, it is the syllable *Om*. That syllable *Om*, while being divided into quarters, is *adhimātram*, exists on letters as its basis. How? Those which constitute the quarters of the Self are the letters of *Om*. Which are they? They are the letters, *a*, *u*, and *m*.

जागरितस्थानो वैश्वानरोऽकारः प्रथमा मात्राऽऽप्तेरादिमत्त्वाद्वाऽऽप्नोति ह वै सर्वान् कामानादिश्च भवति य एवं वेद ॥९॥

9. Vaiśvānara, having the waking state as his sphere, is the first letter *a*, because of (the similarity of) pervasiveness or being the first. He who knows thus, does verily attain all desirable things, and becomes the foremost.

With regard to these, specific relations are being established. He who is *vaiśvānaraḥ*, Vaiśvānara (Virāṭ); *jāgaritasthānaḥ*, with his sphere (of activity) as the waking state;[1] is *akāraḥ*, *a*; *prathamā mātrā*, the first

[1] The Self in the gross individual context (viz Viśva) is identical with the Self in the gross cosmic context (viz Vaiśvānara or Virāṭ). Similarly, it is to be understood that Taijasa is identical with Hiraṇyagarbha, and Prājña with the Unmanifested, the difference lying only in the sphere of manifestation. This identity is suggested by the indiscriminate use of these terms in the present and following texts.

letter, of *Om*. Because of what similarity? That is being said: *Āpteḥ*, because of pervasiveness. *Āpti* means pervasiveness. By the sound *a* is pervaded all speech, according to the Vedic text, 'The sound *a* is indeed all speech' (Ai. Ā. II. iii. 7: 13). Similarly, by Vaiśvānara is pervaded the whole universe, according to the Vedic text, 'Of that very Vaiśvānara-Self who is such, heaven indeed is the head' (Ch. V. xviii. 2). And we said that the word and the thing denoted by the word are the same. That which has *ādi*, precedence, is said to be *ādimat*, first. Just as the letter called *a* is the first, so also is Vaiśvānara. Because of this very similarity Vaiśvānara is identified with *a*. The fruit attained by a knower of this identity is stated: *Āpnoti ha vai sarvān kāmān*, he surely attains all desirable things; *ca bhavati ādiḥ*, and he becomes the foremost, among the great; *yaḥ evam veda*, who knows thus, i.e. knows the identity as stated.

स्वप्नस्थानस्तैजस उकारो द्वितीया मात्रोत्कर्षादुभयत्वाद्वोत्कर्षति ह वै ज्ञानसन्ततिं समानश्च भवति नास्याब्रह्मवित् कुले भवति य एवं वेद ॥१०॥

10. He who is Taijasa with the state of dream as his sphere (of activity) is the second letter *u* (of *Om*); because of the similarity of excellence and intermediateness. He who knows thus increases the current of knowledge and becomes equal to all. None is born in his line who is not a knower of Brahman.

He who is *taijasaḥ*; *svapnasthānaḥ*, with the state of dream as his sphere; is the *dvitīyā mātrā*, second letter; *ukāraḥ*, *u*, of *Om*. Because of what similarity? That is being said: *Utkarṣāt*, because of excellence. The letter *u* is, as it were, better than the letter *a*; so also is Taijasa better than Viśva. *Ubhayatvāt vā*, or (this is so) because of intermediate position. The letter *u* occurs between the letters *a* and *m*; and so also is Taijasa intermediate between Viśva and Prājña. (Taijasa is *u*) because of this similarity of being related to both. The result attained by the knower is being stated: *Utkarṣati ha vai jñānasantatim*, he heightens, that is to say, increases, the current of knowledge; *ca bhavati samānaḥ*, and he becomes equal—he does not become an object of envy to his enemies, as he is not to his friends. *Asya kule*, in the line of this one; *yaḥ evam veda*, who knows thus; *na bhavati abrahmavit*, none is born who is not a knower of Brahman.

सुषुप्तस्थानः प्राज्ञो मकारस्तृतीया मात्रा मितेरपीतेर्वा मिनोति ह वा इदꣳ सर्वमपीतिश्च भवति य एवं वेद ॥११॥

11. Prājña with his sphere of activity in the sleep state is *m*, the third letter of *Om*, because of measuring or because of absorption. Anyone who knows thus measures all this, and he becomes the place of absorption.

He that is *prājñaḥ*, Prājña; *suṣuptasthānaḥ*, with the state of sleep as his sphere; is *makāraḥ*, the letter *m*; which is *tṛtīyā mātrā*, the third letter, of the syllable *Om*. By what analogy? That is being said: This is the analogy here—*miteḥ*, because of measuring. *Miti* means to measure. As barley is measured by the vessel called Prastha, so are Viśva and Taijasa measured, as it were, because of their entry into and coming out of Prājña during dissolution and origination. Similarly, too, at the end of the pronunciation of the syllable *Om* and at the time of its fresh pronunciation, the letters *a* and *u* seem to enter into the last letter *m*, to come out again from it. *Vā apīteḥ*, or because of absorption. *Apīti* means getting merged or united in. At the time of the pronunciation of *Om*, *a* and *u* verily seem to get merged into the last letter *m*. Similarly, Viśva and Taijasa merge into Prājña at the time of sleep. Because of this analogy also there is the identity of Prājña and the letter *m*. The result attained by the man of knowledge is stated: *Minoti ha vai idam sarvam*, he measures all this, that is to say, he knows the reality of the Universe; *ca bhavati apītiḥ*, and he becomes the place of absorption, that is to say, the Self in Its state as the cause of the world. The mention of subsidiary result here is by way of praising the primary means.

GAUḌAPĀDA'S KĀRIKĀ

Here occur these verses (of Gauḍapāda):

विश्वस्यात्वविवक्षायामादिसामान्यमुत्कटम् ।
मात्रासंप्रतिपत्तौ स्यादाप्तिसामान्यमेव च ॥१६॥

19. When the identity of Viśva with the letter *a* is intended, (that is to say) when Viśva's identity with a letter is apprehended, the similarity of being the first, as well as the similarity of all-pervasiveness, emerges in view.

When the identity *viśvasya*, of Viśva; with *a*, with the mere letter *a*, is intended; then, according to the reasoning adduced, *sāmānyam*, the similarity; of being the *ādi*, first; is seen as *utkaṭam*, obvious. This is the idea. The clause 'when the identity with *a* is intended' is explained by *mātrāsaṁpratipattau*, which means 'when Viśva's identity with *a* alone is apprehended'. After '*āpti-sāmānyam eva ca*, the similarity of all-pervasiveness', the word '*utkaṭam*, (is seen as) obvious' is understood because of the use of '*ca*, and'.

तैजसस्योत्वविज्ञान उत्कर्षो दृश्यते स्फुटम् ।
मात्रासंप्रतिपत्तौ स्यादुभयत्वं तथाविधम् ॥२०॥

20. In the matter of comprehending Taijasa as identified with *u*, that is to say, when Taijasa's identity with a letter is apprehended, the similarity of excellence is clearly seen, and intermediacy also is equally clear.

Taijasasya utva-vijñāne, in the matter of knowing Taijasa as the letter *u*, when it is intended to be identified with *u*; *utkarṣaḥ*, excellence; *dṛśyate*, is seen; *sphuṭam*, clearly. This is the meaning. *Ubhayatvam*, intermediacy, is also clear. All this is to be explained as before.

मकारभावे प्राज्ञस्य मानसामान्यमुत्कटम् ।
मात्रासंप्रतिपत्तौ तु लयसामान्यमेव च ॥२१॥

21. In the matter of Prājña's identity with the

letter *m*, that is to say, when Prājña's identity with a letter is apprehended, the similarity of being a measure is seen to emerge plainly, and so also does the similarity of absorption.

The idea is that, in the matter of Prājña's identity with the letter *m*, measurement and absorption are excellent points of similarity.

त्रिषु धामसु यस्तुल्यं सामान्यं वेत्ति निश्चितः ।
स पूज्यः सर्वभूतानां वन्द्यश्चैव महामुनिः ॥२२॥

22. He, the great sage, who knows with firm conviction the common similarities in the three states is worthy of adoration and salutation by all beings.

Saḥ, he, the knower of Brahman; who *niścitaḥ*, with the firm conviction, 'This is certainly so'; *vetti*, knows; in the three states, mentioned above; *tulyam sāmānyam*, the common analogies spoken of; is *pūjyaḥ*, adorable; and *vandyaḥ*, worthy of salutation, in the world.

अकारो नयते विश्वमुकारश्चापि तैजसम् ।
मकारश्च पुनः प्राज्ञं नामात्रे विद्यते गतिः ॥२३॥

23. The letter *a* leads to Viśva; so also the letter *u* leads to Taijasa; and the letter *m*, again, leads to Prājña. (When Prājña disappears) in that (*Om*) which is free from the letters, there remains no attainment.

Akāraḥ, the letter *a*; *nayate*, carries—him who, after

resorting to *Om*, meditates on it by identifying the quarters of the self with the letters of *Om* through the foregoing common features; *viśvam*, to Viśva; makes him attain Viśva. The idea is that he who meditates on *Om* with (emphasis on) *a*, becomes identified with Vaiśvānara (Virāṭ). Similarly, *ukāraḥ*, the letter *u*; takes him *taijasam*, to Taijasa. *Ca*, and; *makāraḥ*, the letter *m*; *punaḥ*, again; *prājñam*, to Prājña. The verb 'leads' is to be understood from the use of the word '*ca*, and'. But when *m*, too, disappears—when the causal state gets destroyed in *Om*; *amātre* which is free from the letters (and parts)—then, *na vidyate*, there does not remain; any *gatiḥ*, attainment.[1]

UPANIṢAD

अमात्रश्चतुर्थोऽव्यवहार्यः प्रपञ्चोपशमः शिवोऽद्वैत एवमोङ्कार आत्मैव संविशत्यात्मनाऽऽत्मानं य एवं वेद ॥१२॥

इति माण्डूक्योपनिषत् समाप्ता ॥

12. The partless *Om* is Turīya—beyond all con-

[1] *A* represents the gross universe, the waking state, and Viśva; *u* represents the subtle universe, dream, and Taijasa; and *m* represents the causal state, sleep, and Prājña. The earlier ones merge into the latter ones. In this way everything is reduced to *Om*. While engaged in this meditation of *Om* as all, there flashes in the aspirant's mind the teacher's insturction that everything is but the absolute Brahman. Then all the phenomenal world, merged in *Om*, disappears in Brahman, and there remains no goal to attain. Though the meditations in the three stages relate to the same *Om*, the results are different in accordance with the emphasis laid on its constituents.

ventional dealings, the limit of the negation of the phenomenal world, the auspicious, and the non-dual. *Om* is thus the Self to be sure. He who knows thus enters the Self through his self.

Amātraḥ, that which has no *mātrā*, part—the partless *Om*; becomes but the *caturthaḥ*, Fourth, Turīya, merely the absolute Self; which is *avyavahāryaḥ*, beyond empirical relations, because of the disappearance of names and nameables, that are but forms of speech and mind; *prapañcopaśamaḥ*, the culmination of phenomenal existence;[1] *śivaḥ*, the auspicious; and *advaitaḥ*, non-dual. *Evam*, thus; *Om*, as possessed of the three letters and as applied by a man with the above knowledge, is *ātmā eva*, verily identical with the Self possessed of three quarters. *Yaḥ evam veda*, he who knows thus; *saṁviśati*, enters; *ātmānam*, into (his own supreme) Self; *ātmanā*, through (his own) self. The knower of Brahman, who has realized the highest Truth, has entered into the Self by burning away the third state of latency; and hence he is not born again, since Turīya has no latency (of creation). For when a snake superimposed on a rope has merged in the rope on the discrimination of the rope and the snake, it does not appear again to those discriminating people, just as before, from the impressions (of the past persisting) in the intellect. To those men of renunciation, however, who are possessed of dull or average intellect, who still consider themselves aspirants, who tread the virtuous path, and who know the common features

[1] The ultimate limit of the negation of the world.

of the letters and the quarters (of *Om* and the Self) as presented before, (to them) the syllable *Om*, when meditated on in the proper way, becomes helpful for the realization of Brahman. In support of this it will be said, 'There are three stages of life—inferior,' etc. (*Kārikā*, III. 16).

GAUḌAPĀDA'S KĀRIKĀ

Just as before, here occur these verses:

ओङ्कारं पादशो विद्यात्पादा मात्रा न संशयः ।
ओङ्कारं पादशो ज्ञात्वा न किंचिदपि चिन्तयेत् ॥२४॥

24. One should know *Om*, quarter by quarter; (for) there is no doubt that the quarters (of the Self) are the letters (of *Om*). Having known *Om*, quarter by quarter, one should not think of anything whatsoever.

Because of the aforesaid similarity, the quarters are the letters, and the letters are the quarters. Therefore *vidyāt*, one should know; *oṅkāram*, the syllable *Om*; *pādaśaḥ*, quarter by quarter. This is the meaning. When the syllable *Om* is known thus, *na cintayet*, one should not think of; *kim cit api*, anything whatsoever, serving any seen or unseen purpose; for he has got all his desires fulfilled.

युञ्जीत प्रणवे चेतः प्रणवो ब्रह्म निर्भयम् ।
प्रणवे नित्ययुक्तस्य न भयं विद्यते क्वचित् ॥२५॥

25. One should concentrate one's mind on *Om*, (for) *Om* is Brahman, beyond fear. For a man, ever fixed in Brahman, there can be no fear anywhere.

Yuñjīta, one should concentrate; *cetaḥ*, the mind; *praṇave*, on *Om*, as explained, which is essentially the supreme Reality; for *praṇavaḥ*, *Om*; is *brahma nirbhayam*, Brahman beyond fear; because for one who is ever fixed in it, *na bhayam vidyate kvacit*, there can be no fear anywhere, in accordance with the Vedic text, 'The enlightened man is not afraid of anything' (Tai. II. ix).

प्रणवो ह्यपरं ब्रह्म प्रणवश्च परः स्मृतः।
अपूर्वोऽनन्तरोऽबाह्योऽनपरः प्रणवोऽव्ययः ॥२६॥

26. *Om* is surely the inferior Brahman; and *Om* is considered to be the superior Brahman. *Om* is without cause, without inside and outside, and without effect; and it is undecaying.

Praṇavaḥ, *Om*, is both the superior and inferior Brahman. When the quarters and letters disappear, from the highest standpoint, *Om* becomes verily the supreme Self that is Brahman. Therefore it is *apūrvaḥ*, without any cause preceding it. There is nothing inside it that is of a different class; therefore it is *anantaraḥ*, without inside. Similarly, there is nothing existing outside; therefore it is *abāhyaḥ*, without outside. There is no effect (*aparam*) of it; therefore it is *anaparaḥ*, without effect. The idea implied (as a whole) is that it is coextensive with all that is inside or outside; it is verily birthless; and it is a mass of Consciousness, homogeneous like a lump of salt.

सर्वस्य प्रणवो ह्यादिर्मध्यमन्तस्तथैव च ।
एवं हि प्रणवं ज्ञात्वा व्यश्नुते तदनन्तरम् ॥२७॥

27. *Om* is indeed the beginning, middle, and end of everything. Having known *Om* in this way indeed one attains immediately (identity with the Self).

Just like the magician and others, (*Om* is the) beginning (*ādi*), middle (*madhya*), and end (*anta*) — the origination, continuance, and dissolution; *sarvasya*, of all — of the whole phenomenal universe, consisting of space and the rest which originate like a magic elephant, a snake superimposed in a rope, a mirage, a dream, etc. (from the magician and the rest). *Evam hi*, in this way indeed; *jñātvā praṇavam*, having known *Om*, which is the Self and comparable to the magician and the rest; *vyaśnute*, one attains — identity with the Self, at that very moment. This is the idea.

प्रणवं हीश्वरं विद्यात् सर्वस्य हृदि संस्थितम् ।
सर्वव्यापिनमोङ्कारं मत्वा धीरो न शोचति ॥२८॥

28. One should know *Om*, to be God seated in the hearts of all. Meditating on the all-pervasive *Om*, the intelligent man grieves no more.

Vidyāt, one should know; *praṇavam*, *Om*; as *īśvaram*, God; existing *hṛdi*, in the heart — the seat of memory and perception—of all living beings. *Matvā*, having meditated on (i.e. realized); *oṅkāram*, *Om*, which is the Self beyond the worldly state; and *sarvavyāpinam*, all-pervasive, like space; *dhīraḥ*, the intelligent man; *na śocati*, does not grieve; for no cause of grief can be possible (then)—in accordance with such Vedic texts as, 'A knower of the Self transcends sorrow' (Ch. VII. i. 3).

अमात्रोऽनन्तमात्रश्च द्वैतस्योपशमः शिवः ।
ओङ्कारो विदितो येन स मुनिर्नेतरो जनः ॥२९॥

29. The *Om*, without measures and possessed of infinite dimension, is the auspicious entity where all duality ceases. He by whom *Om* is known, is the real sage, and not so is any other man.

Amātraḥ, (*Om*) beyond measures, is Turīya. *Mātrā*, derived in the sense of that by which anything is measured, signifies dimension; that which has infinite (*ananta*) dimension is *anantamātraḥ*; the idea is that its extension cannot be determined. It is *śivaḥ*, auspicious, holy, because it is the state of negation of all duality. *Saḥ yena*, he by whom; *oṅkāraḥ*, *Om*, as explained; *viditaḥ*, is known; is a *muniḥ*, sage (lit. a meditator), because of his meditating on the supreme Reality. *Na itaraḥ janaḥ*, not any other man, even though he may be learned in the scriptures. This is the idea.

CHAPTER II

VAITATHYA-PRAKARAṆA (ON UNREALITY)

In consonance with such Vedic text as, 'One only, without a second' (Ch. VI. ii. 1), it has been said that duality ceases to exist after realization (*Kārikā*, I. 18). That is, however, only a scriptural assertion. But this falsity can be confirmed even through reasoning. This is why the second chapter (of the *Kārikā*) commences:

वैतथ्यं सर्वभावानां स्वप्न आहुर्मनीषिणः ।
अन्तःस्थानात्तु भावानां संवृतत्वेन हेतुना ॥१॥

1. The wise declare the falsity of all objects in a dream because of the location of the objecls inside (the body) and by reason of (the space) being small.

The state of the *vitatha*, unreal, is *vaitathyam*, unreality, or falsity. Of what? *Sarvabhāvānām*, of all objects, both external and internal; that are perceived *svapne*, in dream. (This is what) *manīṣiṇaḥ*, the wise people, adept in the use of the means of knowledge; *āhuḥ*, say. The ground of falsity is being stated: *antaḥ-sthānāt*, because of existence inside; because of those (*bhāvāḥ*, things) having their *sthāna*, place; *antaḥ*, inside the body; for objects (*bhāvāḥ*) such as elephants or mountains, are perceived there and not outside the body. Therefore they ought to be false.

Objection: This ground of inference (viz existence within) is invalidated by the perception of (real) jars etc. within a house etc.[1]

In *answer* to this objection it is said: *saṁvṛtatvena hetunā*, by reason of being small, that is to say, because of the small (-ness of the) space confined within (the body). For mountains and elephants cannot possibly exist within the limited space inside the nerves in the (dreamer's) body. A mountain does not surely exist within a body.

Objection: It is not tenable that the things seen in a dream have a limited space inside (the body); for one sleeping in the east is seen as though dreaming in the north.

Apprehending such an objection the text answers:

अदीर्घत्वाच्च कालस्य गत्वा देशान्न पश्यति।
प्रतिबुद्धश्च वै सर्वस्तस्मिन्देशे न विद्यते ॥२॥

2. Besides, one does not see places by going there, for the time is not long enough. Moreover every dreamer, when awakened, does not continue in that place (of dream).

One does not dream by going anywhere outside the body; for as soon as one goes to sleep, one sees as though one is dreaming in a place eight hundred miles

[1] So, 'existence within' is no valid ground for inferring that a thing is unreal.

away from the body that can be reached in a month only. Neither is there sufficient time to reach there and come back. Hence *adīrghatvāt ca kālasya*, inasmuch as the time is not long enough, the dreamer does not go to a different place. Moreover, *pratibuddhaḥ ca vai sarvaḥ*, every dreamer, when awakened; *na vidyate*, does not stay, in the places dreamt of. Should one go to a different region in dream, one should wake up in the region of one's dream. But this is not a fact. A man sleeping at night, sees things as though in the day time. And when the dreamer comes into contact with many, he should be acknowledged as such by those whom he meets. But he is not apprehended thus; for if they really contacted him, they would say, 'We noticed you there today.' But this is not so. Therefore he does not go to a different place in dream.

Things seen in a dream are unreal because of this further reason:

अभावश्च रथादीनां श्रूयते न्यायपूर्वकम् ।
वैतथ्यं तेन वै प्राप्तं स्वप्न आहुः प्रकाशितम् ॥३॥

3. Besides, the absence of chariot etc. is heard of in the Upaniṣad from the standpoint of logic. They say that the falsity arrived at thus (by logic) is reiterated by the Upaniṣad in the context of dream.

Ca, besides; *abhāvaḥ*, non-existence; *rathādīnām*, of chariots etc; *śrūyate*, is heard of in the Upaniṣad, in the text, 'There are no chariots, nor animals to be yoked to them' (Bṛ. IV. iii. 10); *nyāyapūrvakam*, from the standpoint of logic. They, the knowers of Brahman, *āhuḥ*, say; that the *vaitathyam*, unreality; *prāptam*, arrived at; through such reasons as existence inside the body, smallness of the space, etc.; is *prakāśitam*, revealed by the Upaniṣad, which reiterates that fact while engaged in establishing (the soul's) self-effulgence; *svapne*, in dream.

अन्तःस्थानात्तु भेदानां तस्माज्जागरिते स्मृतम् ।
यथा तत्र तथा स्वप्ने संवृतत्वेन भिद्यते ॥४॥

4. As the dream-objects are unreal in a dream, so also, because of that very reason, the objects in the waking state are unreal. But objects (in the dream state) differ because of existence inside (the body) and because of the smallness (of space).

The proposition (major premiss) to be established is the unreality of objects seen in the waking state. 'Being perceived' is the ground of inference (middle term). And the illustration (in confirmation) is 'like an object seen in a dream'. And the assertion of the presence of the middle term in the minor term is made thus: *Yathā tatra svapne*, as (objects 'perceived') there in a dream, are false; so also are they false *jāgarite*, in the waking state; the fact of 'being perceived' being equally present. And the concluding reiteration is: *Tasmāt jāgarite smṛtam*, therefore falsity is admitted of objects in the waking state as well. The difference of the dream-objects from the objects of the waking state is *antaḥsthānāt*, because of the former being confined within; and *saṁvṛtatvena*, because of the smallness (of space). And the common features in both the states are the facts of being perceived and being false.

स्वप्नजागरितस्थाने ह्येकमाहुर्मनीषिणः ।
भेदानां हि समत्वेन प्रसिद्धेनैव हेतुना ।।५।।

5. Inasmuch as the diverse things are (found to be) similar on the strength of the familiar ground of inference, the wise say that the dream and the waking states are one.

Samatvena, inasmuch as there is similarity; *bhedā-nām*, of the diverse things; *prasiddhena eva hetunā*, on the strength of the familiar ground of inference, viz that things (in dream and waking states) are equally related as the perceiver and the perceived;[1] therefore the discriminating people speak of the sameness of the states of waking and dream. This is only a corollary of what was arrived at through the earlier means of proof.

आदावन्ते च यन्नास्ति वर्तमानेऽपि तत्तथा ।
वितथैः सदृशाः सन्तोऽवितथा इव लक्षिताः ।।६।।

6. That which does not exist in the beginning and the end is equally so in the present (i.e in the middle). Though they are on the same footing with the unreal, yet they are seen as though real.

The different things noticed in the waking state are

[1]On the logical ground of 'being perceived'.

unreal for this additional reason that they do not exist in the beginning and at the end. A thing, for instance a mirage, *yat*, which; *na asti*, does not exist; *ādau ante ca*, in the beginning and at the end; *tat*, that; does not exist even in the middle. This is the ascertained truth in the world. So also these different things seen in the waking state are indeed unreal, they being *vitathaiḥ sadṛśāḥ*, similar to, (on the same footing with), unreal things like the mirage etc., on account of their non-existence in the beginning and at the end. And yet *avitathāḥ iva lakṣitāḥ*, they are perceived as though real, by the ignorant who do not know the Self.

Objection: The assertion that the things seen in the waking state are unreal like those seen in the dream is wrong, since objects of the waking state, for instance food, drink, vehicles, etc., are seen to fulfil some purpose by assuaging hunger and thirst and by moving to and fro, whereas dream objects have no such utility. Therefore it is a mere figment of the brain to say that the objects of the waking state are illusory like those of dream.

Answer: That is not so.

Objection: Why?

Answer: Because:

सप्रयोजनता तेषां स्वप्ने विप्रतिपद्यते।
तस्मादाद्यन्तवत्त्वेन मिथ्यैव खलु ते स्मृताः ॥७॥

7. Their utility is contradicted in dream. There-

fore from the fact of their having a beginning and an end they are rightly held to be unreal.

Saprayojanatā, the utility, which is noticed (in the waking state), of food, drink, etc.; *vipratipadyate svapne*, is contradicted in dream. For a man who has got his hunger appeased and thirst quenched by eating and drinking in the waking state, as soon as he goes to sleep, feels as though he is afflicted by hunger, thirst, etc. and has been fasting for a whole day and night. This is similar to the case where, after getting full satisfaction in dream from eating and drinking, he wakes up to feel hunger and thirst. Therefore the objects of the waking state are seen to be contradicted in dream. Accordingly, we are of the opinion that their unreality like that of dream-objects is beyond doubt. Hence from the fact that they possess the common feature of having a beginning and an end, they are rightly held to be unreal.

Objection: From the fact of the similarity of the diverse things in the dream and the waking states, it is wrong to assert that the diversities seen in the waking state are illusory.

Counter-objection: Why?

Opponent: Because the illustration is inapplicable.

Counter-objection: How?

Opponent: For, these very same objects seen in the waking state are not experienced in dream.

Counter-objection: What are they then?

Opponent: One sees something novel in a dream. One thinks oneself to be possessed of eight arms and sitting astride an elephant with four tusks. Similarly, too, one sees other grotesque things in a dream. That being dissimilar to any other unreal thing must be true. So the analogy is inapt. Hence it is illogical to say that the waking state is false like dream.

Vedāntin: That is not so. The uniqueness that is supposed by you to be seen in a dream is not so by its own right.

Opponent: How is it then?

अपूर्वं स्थानिधर्मो हि यथा स्वर्गनिवासिनाम् ।
तानयं प्रेक्षते गत्वा यथैवेह सुशिक्षितः ॥८॥

8. The unique attribute is a mere attribute of the experiencer in a particular state, as it is in the case of the dwellers in heaven. This he experiences by going there, just as one, well informed, does in this world.

Apūrvam, the novel attribute; *hi sthānidharmaḥ*, is a mere quality (*dharma*) of (*sthānī*) the man in a certain state, viz the experiencer in the state of dream; *yathā svarganivāsinām*, as it is with the dwellers of heaven, Indra and others, who have such attributes as the possession of a thousand eyes, and so on.[1] Similarly is this a novel attribute of the dreamer; but it is not there by its own right like the real nature of the seer.

[1] Men who become gods, get such experiences.

Tān, these, the unique things of this kind that are creations of his mind; *ayam*, this one, the man in that state, the dreamer; *prekṣate*, sees; *gatvā*, by going, to the dream state. As *iha*, in this world; *suśikṣitaḥ*, a man well informed about the way leading to another region, goes along that way to that other region and sees those objects, so is the case here. Hence, just as the appearances of things in certain states, such as a snake on a rope or a mirage in a desert, are unreal, similarly the novelties experienced in a dream are merely attributes of the dreamer in that state; and therefore they are unreal. Accordingly, the analogy of the dream is not inapplicable.

The assumption of uniqueness in the illustration of dream has been demolished. Now the *Kārikā* again proceeds by way of dilating on the similarity of objects of the waking and dream states:

स्वप्नवृत्तावपि त्वन्तश्चेतसा कल्पितं त्वसत् ।
बहिश्चेतोगृहीतं सद्दृष्टं वैतथ्यमेतयोः ॥९॥

9. Even in the dream state itself, anything imagined by the inner consciousness is unreal, while anything experienced by the outer consciousness is real. (But) both these are seen to be false.

Svapnavṛttau api, even in the dream state; anything experienced *antaścetasā*, by the internal consciousness, anything called up by our fancy; is *asat*, unreal, since it ceases to be perceived the very moment after being imagined. In that very dream again, whatever is perceived, for instance a pot, which was (earlier) *gṛhītam*, perceived; *bahiścetasā*, by external consciousness, through the eye etc., is *sat*, real. Thus, though it is definitely known that dream experiences are false, still a division of true and false is seen there. Nevertheless, *vaitathyam dṛṣṭam*, unreality is perceived, for both kinds of things, be they imagined by inner or outer consciousness.

जाग्रद्वृत्तावपि त्वन्तश्चेतसा कल्पितं त्वसत् ।
बहिश्चेतोगृहीतं सद्युक्तं वैतथ्यमेतयोः ॥१०॥

10. Even in the waking state, whatever is imagined by the inner consciousness is false and whatever is perceived by the outer consciousness is true. It is reasonable that both these should be unreal.

It is reasonable to say that both the (so-called) true and false are unreal, for they are equally imagined either by the internal or external consciousness. The remaining portion is as already explained.

The *opponent* says:

उभयोरपि वैतथ्यं भेदानां स्थानयोर्यदि ।
क एतान् बुध्यते भेदान् को वै तेषां विकल्पकः ॥११॥

11. If all objects in both the states be unreal, who apprehends these objects and who indeed is their creator?

Yadi, if; there be *vaitathyam*, unreality; *bhedānām*,

of the objects; *sthānayoḥ*, in the two—waking and dream—states; then *kaḥ*, who; is it that *budhyate*, cognizes; *etān*, these, which are imagined inside and outside the mind; and *kaḥ vai teṣām vikalpakaḥ*, who is indeed their (imaginer,) creator? The idea implied is this: If you do not want to adopt a theory of the non-existence of the Self, (and want to posit something behind phenomena), then who is the support of memory and knowledge?

(The *answer* is:)

कल्पयत्यात्मनाऽऽत्मानमात्मा देवः स्वमायया ।
स एव बुध्यते भेदानिति वेदान्तनिश्चयः ॥१२॥

12. The self-effulgent Self imagines Itself through Itself by the power of Its own Māyā. The Self Itself cognizes the objects. Such is the definite conclusion of Vedānta.

Svamāyayā, through Its own Māyā; *devaḥ ātmā*, the self-effulgent Self Itself; *kalpayati*, imagines; Its own *ātmānam*, Self, in the Self Itself, to be possessed of different forms to be spoken of later, just as snakes etc. are imagined on rope etc. And in the very same way It Itself *budhyate*, cognizes; those *bhedān*, objects; *iti*, such; is *vedāntaniścayaḥ*, the definite conclusion of Vedānta. There is nothing else (but the Self) as the support of cognition and memory; nor are cognition and memory without support as is held by the Nihilists. This is the idea.

While imagining, in what way does the Self do so? This is being answered:

विकरोत्यपरान्भावानन्तश्चित्ते व्यवस्थितान् ।
नियतांश्च बहिश्चित्त एवं कल्पयते प्रभुः ॥१३॥

13. The Lord manifests diversely the mundane things existing in the mind. Turning the mind outward, He creates the well-defined things (as well as the undefined things). Thus does the Lord imagine.

(*Prabhuḥ*, the Lord); *vikaroti*, manifests diversely; *aparān*, the non-transcendental, mundane; *bhāvān*, objects, such as sound and other unmanifested objects; *vyavasthitān*, existing; *antaścitte*, inside the mind, in the form of impressions and tendencies. And *bahiścittaḥ* (*san*), having the mind turned outward; (the Lord manifests diversely) *niyatān*, things well-defined, such as the earth etc.—as also those not well-defined, that exist so long as the imagination lasts. Similarly (He manifests diversely) such things as mental desires by making His mind turn inward. *Evam*, in this way; *prabhuḥ*, the Lord, God, that is to say, the Self, imagines.

The assertion that everything is a subjective creation like dream is questioned, for, unlike the subjective creations, to wit, desire etc., that are circumscribed by the mind, the external objects are mutually determined.

That doubt is unreasonable, (for—)

चित्तकाला हि येऽन्तस्तु द्वयकालाश्च ये बहिः ।
कल्पिता एव ते सर्वे विशेषो नान्यहेतुकः ॥१४॥

14. Things that exist internally as long as the thought lasts and things that are externally related to two points of time, are all imaginations. Their distinction is not caused by anything else.

Cittakālāḥ hi ye antaḥ tu, things that exist internally as long as the thought lasts: those that are circumscribed by the mind thought and those that have no time for determining them apart from the time for which their thought lasts are *cittakālāḥ*, existing as long as the thought lasts. The idea is that they are apprehended only during the time of their imagination. *Dvayakālāḥ*, those that are possessed of two times, i.e. which are related to different times, which are mutually determined. As for instance, 'He stays during the milking', which means that the cow is milked as long as he stays, and he stays as long as the cow is milked. 'This one lasts for that time'; 'That one lasts for this time'—thus, external factors mutually determine each other. They are thus related to two points of time. Whether they be subjective, lasting for the time of the thought, or objective, related to two points of time, *kalpitā eva te sarve*, they are all but fancies. The fact that external objects have the distinction of being related to two points of time, *na anya hetukaḥ*, has no other reason but that of being imagined. Here, too, the illustration of dream fits in.

अव्यक्ता एव येऽन्तस्तु स्फुटा एव च ये बहिः ।
कल्पिता एव ते सर्वे विशेषस्त्विन्द्रियान्तरे ॥१५॥

15. Those objects that appear indistinct inside the

mind, and those that appear vivid outside, are all merely created by imagination. Their distinction is to be traced to the difference in the organs of perception.

The fact that things in the mind, called up by mere mental impressions, have an indistinctness, while externally, as objects of the sense of sight etc., they have a vividness, (that fact) is not due to the existence of the objects themselves; for this distinction is noticed even in dream. To what is it due then? This is caused by the difference in the organs of perception. Hence it is proved that the things of the waking state are as much a creation of imagination as the dream objects.

What is the root of imagining that the external and the mental objects are mutually related by way of causation? The answer is:

जीवं कल्पयते पूर्वं ततो भावान् पृथग्विधान् ।
बाह्यानाध्यात्मिकांश्चैव यथाविद्यस्तथास्मृतिः ॥१६॥

16. First He imagines the individual (soul) and then He imagines the different objects, external and mental. The individual gets his memory in accordance with the kind of thought-impressions he has.

Like the fancying of a snake in a rope, He *pūrvam kalpayate*, first imagines; *jīvam*, the individual—who is a bundle of causes and effects expressing themselves through such beliefs as, 'I act; and mine are the (resulting) sorrows and happiness'—on the pure Self that is devoid of such characteristics. After that, for his sake, He (the Lord) imagines different objects, such as the vital force and so on, *bāhyān ādhyātmikān ca eva*, both external and mental, dividing them into action, instruments, and results. As to that, what is the reason for that imagination? That is being stated. The individual that is imagined by (the Lord) Himself and is himself capable of imagination, gets a memory, *yathāvidyaḥ*, in accordance with the kind of thought-impressions that he is possessed of; that fact is alluded to by *tathāsmṛtiḥ*, he is possessed of that kind of memory. Hence, from the apprehension of some fancy as the cause, there follows the apprehension of the result;[1] from that (awareness of causal relation) follows the memory of the cause and the effect, and from that follows their apprehension, as well as the awareness of the action and accessories that this apprehension of causality leads to, and the awareness of the different results following from those actions etc.[2] From their awareness arises their memory; and from that memory again arises their awareness. In this way He imagines diversely the things, both external and mental to be mutually the causes and effects.

In the previous verse it has been said that the im-

[1] If there is eating and drinking, there follows satisfaction; if eating and drinking are absent, satisfaction is wanting; from this the fancy follows that eating etc. are the causes of satisfaction.

[2] From the above awareness follows memory on another occasion; from that arises the awareness of the need of action with regard to similar factors that are supposed to lead to satisfaction; from that follows cooking, getting of rice, and producing the result.

agining of individuality is the root of all other imaginations. Through an illustration is being shown what that imagining of an individual soul is due to:

अनिश्चिता यथा रज्जुरन्धकारे विकल्पिता।
सर्पधारादिभिर्भावैस्तद्वदात्मा विकल्पितः ॥१७॥

17. As a rope whose nature has not been well ascertained is imagined in the dark to be various things like a snake, a line of water, etc., so also is the Self imagined variously.

As it happens in common experience, that a *rajjuḥ*, rope; that is *aniścitā*, not well ascertained, in its true reality as 'This is so indeed'; is *vikalpitā*, imagined variously, in hazy darkness, as a snake, a line of water, or a stick, just because its real nature has not been determined earlier—for if the rope had been ascertained earlier in its own essence, there would not have been such imaginations as of a snake etc., as for instance, there is no such imagination with regard to the fingers in one's own hands; this is the illustration—similarly, the Self is imagined to be such countless diverse objects as an individual creature or the vital force etc., just because It has not been ascertained in Its true nature to be pure intelligence, existence, and non-duality, and different from such evils as cause and effect that are the characteristics of the world. This is the conclusion of all the Upaniṣads.

निश्चितायां यथा रज्ज्वां विकल्पो विनिवर्तते।
रज्जुरेवेति चाद्वैतं तद्वदात्मविनिश्चयः ॥१८॥

18. As illusion (on the rope) ceases and the rope alone remains when the rope is ascertained to be nothing but the rope, so also is the ascertainment about the Self.

As on the ascertainment that it is *rajjuḥ eva*, nothing but a rope, all the imaginations disappear and there remains the rope alone without anything else, so also from the scriptural text, 'Not this, not this' (Bṛ. IV. iv. 22), establishing the Self as devoid of all worldly attributes, there dawns, as a result of the light of the sun of realization, this *ātma-viniścayaḥ*, firm conviction about the Self, viz 'the Self indeed is all this' (Ch. VII. xxv. 2), (the Self is) 'without anterior or posterior, without interior or exterior' (Bṛ. II. v. 19), 'since He is coextensive with all that is external and internal and since He is birthless' (Mu. II. i. 2), 'Undecaying, immortal, undying, fearless' (Bṛ. IV. iv. 25), 'One only, without a second' (Ch. VI. ii. 1).

If it be a well ascertained truth that the Self is but one, why is It imagined as so many of these infinite things like the vital force etc. that constitute phenomenal existence? To this hear the answer:

प्राणादिभिरनन्तैश्च भावैरेतैर्विकल्पितः ।
मायैषा तस्य देवस्य यया संमोहितः स्वयम् ॥१९॥

19. (This Self) is imagined to be the infinite objects like Prāṇa (the vital force) etc. This is the Māyā of that self-effulgent One, by which He Himself is deluded.

Eṣā māyā, this is the Māyā; *tasya devasya*, of that self-effulgent Self. As the magical spell created by the magician makes the very clear sky appear as though filled with leafy trees in bloom, similar is this Māyā of the self-effulgent One, by which He Himself seems to have become influenced like a man under delusion. It has been said, 'My Māyā is difficult to get over' (G. VII. 14).

प्राण इति प्राणविदो भूतानीति च तद्विदः ।
गुणा इति गुणविदस्तत्त्वानीति च तद्विदः ॥२०॥

20. Those who know Prāṇa[1] consider Prāṇa (to be the reality). The knowers of the elements consider the elements to be so,[2] the knowers of the qualities (*guṇas*) cling to the qualities,[3] and the knowers of the categories swear by them.[4]

पादा इति पादविदो विषया इति तद्विदः ।
लोका इति लोकविदो देवा इति च तद्विदः ॥२१॥

21. The knowers of the quarters (viz Viśva, Taijasa, and Prājña) consider the quarters to be the reality.

[1] Hiraṇyagarbha or the immanent God. This is the view of the worshippers of Hiraṇyagarbha and of the Vaiśeṣikas.

[2] The Lokāyata materialists swear by the four elements — earth, water, fire, and air.

[3] The Sāṁkhyas hold to Sattva, Rajas, and Tamas, which are the constituents (*guṇas*, lit. qualities) of Prakṛti.

[4] The Śaivas hold that the three categories — Self, ignorance, and Śiva — are the source of the world.

The knowers of the sense-objects[1] consider the sense-objects to be so. According to the knowers of the worlds, the worlds constitute reality.[2] And the worshippers of the gods stand by the gods.

वेदा इति वेदविदो यज्ञा इति च तद्विदः ।
भोक्तेति च भोक्तृविदो भोज्यमिति च तद्विदः ॥२२॥

22. The Vedic scholars ascribe reality to the Vedas, while the sacrificers[3] ascribe this to the sacrifices. Those acquainted with the enjoyer consider it to be the reality,[4] whereas those[5] conversant with the enjoyable things consider them to be so.

सूक्ष्म इति सूक्ष्मविदः स्थूल इति च तद्विदः ।
मूर्त इति मूर्तविदोऽमूर्त इति च तद्विदः ॥२३॥

23. People conversant with the subtle consider reality also to be so, while others dealing with the gross consider it to be so. The worshippers of God with forms consider reality as possessed of forms,[6] whereas those[7] who swear by formlessness call it a void.

[1] The followers of Vātsyāyana and others.

[2] The Paurāṇikas understand the earth, the intermediate world and heaven to be eternal realities.

[3] Like Baudhāyana.

[4] The Sāṁkhya view is that the Self is an enjoyer but not an agent of work.

[5] The cooks.

[6] E.g. Śiva or Viṣṇu.

[7] The Nihilists.

काल इति कालविदो दिश इति च तद्विदः।
वादा इति वादविदो भुवनानीति तद्विदः ॥२४॥

24. The calculators of time (the astrologers) call it time. The knowers of the directions consider them real. The dabblers in theories[1] accept these to be so. And the knowers of the universe consider the (fourteen) worlds to be so.

मन इति मनोविदो बुद्धिरिति च तद्विदः।
चित्तमिति चित्तविदो धर्माधर्मौ च तद्विदः ॥२५॥

25. The knowers[2] of the mind call it the Self, whereas the knowers[3] of intelligence take it for the reality. The knowers[4] of ideas consider them to be the reality. And the knowers[5] of virtue and vice attribute reality to them.

पञ्चविंशक इत्येके षड्विंश इति चापरे।
एकत्रिंशक इत्याहुरनन्त इति चापरे ॥२६॥

26. Some[6] say that reality is constituted by twenty-

[1] That the metals, *mantras*, etc. hold in them the secret of immortality.

[2] A class of materialists.

[3] A class of Buddhists.

[4] The Buddhists who swear by subjective ideas which have no corresponding external things.

[5] The Mīmāṁsakas.

[6] The Puruṣa (the conscious individual soul), Pradhāna or Prakṛti (Nature), Mahat (intelligence), Ahaṁkāra (egoism), the five subtle elements, five senses of perception, five organs of action, five sense-objects, and mind. This is the Sāṁkhya view.

five principles, while others[1] speak of twenty-six. Some[2] say that it consists of thirty-one categories, while according to others they are infinite.

लोकाँल्लोकविदः प्राहुराश्रमा इति तद्विदः।
स्त्रीपुंनपुंसकं लैङ्गाः परापरमथापरे ॥२७॥

27. Adepts in human dealings say that the people (that is to say, people's pleasures) are the real things. Persons conversant with the stages of life hold those to be the reality. The grammarians hold the view that words belonging to the masculine, feminine, and neuter genders are the reality; while others know reality to be constituted by the higher and lower (Brahmans).

सृष्टिरिति सृष्टिविदो लय इति च चद्विदः।
स्थितिरिति स्थितिविदः सर्वे चेह तु सर्वदा ॥२८॥

28. People conversant with creation call creation to be the reality. The knowers of dissolution call it dissolution. The knowers of subsistence call it subsistence. All these ideas are for ever imagined on the Self.

(20-28.) Prāṇa means Prājña, the Self in the state of latency. Everything else, ending with subsistence,

[1] The above 25 and God, according to Patañjali.
[2] The Pāśupatas add *rāga* (attachment), *avidyā* (ignorance), *niyati* (fate), *kālakalā* (divisions of time), and Māyā (cosmic illusion) to the above 26.

is only His product. And similarly all other popular ideas, conceived by every being, like a snake etc. on a rope, are mere imaginations on the Self that is devoid of all of them; and these are caused by ignorance consisting in the non-determination of the nature of the Self. This is the purport (of these verses) as a whole. No attempt is made to explain each of the words in the verses starting with the word Prāṇa, since this is of little practical value and since the meanings of the terms are clear.

यं भावं दर्शयेद्यस्य तं भावं स तु पश्यति।
तं चावति स भूत्वाऽसौ तद्ग्रहः समुपैति तम् ॥२९॥

29. Anyone to whom a teacher may show a particular object (as the reality) sees that alone. And that thing, too, protects him by becoming identified with him. That absorption leads to his self-identity (with the object of attention).

To be brief, *yasya*, anyone to whom; a teacher or any other trustworthy person; *darśayet*, may show; any *bhāvam*, positive object, enumerated or not, from among such things as Prāṇa and the rest, by saying, 'This is verily the reality'; *saḥ*, he (that instructed man); *paśyati*, sees; *tam bhāvam*, that object, by identifying it with himself as either 'I am this' or 'This is mine'. *Ca*, and; *saḥ*, that, that object that was shown; *avati*, protects; *tam*, him, that seer; *asau bhūtvā*, by becoming one with him; that is to say, that object occupies his attention to the exclusion of all others and keeps him confined within itself. *Tadgrahaḥ* means the state of being taken up with that, absorption in it under the idea, 'This is the reality'. The absorption, (*samupaiti*) *tam*, approaches him, viz the one who has accepted (the thing); that is to say, it culminates in identification with him.

एतैरेषोऽपृथग्भावैः पृथगेवेति लक्षितः।
एवं यो वेद तत्त्वेन कल्पयेत् सोऽविशङ्कितः ॥३०॥

30. Through these things that are (really) non-different (from the Self), this One is presented as though really different. He who truly knows this grasps (the meaning of the Vedas) without any hesitation.

Etaiḥ, through these, viz Prāṇa, etc; *apṛthagbhāvaiḥ*, through these things that are non-different—from the Self; *eṣaḥ*, this One, the Self; *lakṣitaḥ*, is pointed out, is believed in by the ignorant; *pṛthak eva iti*, as though really different, just as a rope is considered to be diverse imaginary things like snake etc. This is the meaning. The idea is this: Just as to the discriminating people, the snake etc. do not exist apart from the rope, so also Prāṇa etc. have no existence apart from the Self. And this is in accord with the Vedic text, 'All these are (but) the Self' (Bṛ. II. iv. 6). *Yaḥ veda*, he who knows; *evam* thus; *tattvena*, truly—knows from Vedic texts and from reasoning, that all things imagined on the Self are unreal apart from the Self, like the snake imagined in the rope, and knows that the Self is transcendental and untouched by illusion; *saḥ*, he; *kalpayet*, (i.e. *kalpayati*), grasps, the meanings of the Vedas in their respective contexts; *aviśaṅkitaḥ*, without any hesitation; he understands that a certain passage means this and a certain other means that. None but a knower of the Self can understand truly the purport of the Vedas. Thus indeed is the statement of Manu: '. . . none but a knower of the Self can derive any benefit from the valid means of knowledge'[1] (M. VI. 82).

It is being stated that this unreality of duality that has been established logically is also derived from the valid evidence of Vedānta:

स्वप्नमाये यथा दृष्टे गन्धर्वनगरं यथा।
तथा विश्वमिदं दृष्टं वेदान्तेषु विचक्षणैः ॥३१॥

31. Just as dream and magic are seen to be unreal, or as is a city in the sky, so also is this whole universe known to be unreal from the Upaniṣads by the wise.

Svapna-māye, dream and magic, though unreal, being constituted by unreal things, are considered by the non-discriminating people to be constituted by real things. Again, just as *gandharvanagaram*, an illusory city in the sky—appearing to be full of shops replete with vendable articles, houses, palaces, and villages

[1] This is Ānanda Giri's interpretation of the word *kriyāphala*, where *kriyā* (action) stands for any valid means of knowledge; and its *phala* (result) is the knowledge of Reality; for, even *kriyā* in the sense of Vedic rites etc. is meant to serve the purpose of Illumination by purifying the aspirant's heart.

bustling with men and women—is seen to vanish suddenly before one's very eyes; or just as the *svapna-māye*, dream and magic; *dṛṣṭe*, are seen—to be unreal; *tathā*, similarly; *idam viśvam*, this whole universe, this entire duality; *dṛṣṭam*, is viewed, as unreal. Where? That is being stated. *Vedānteṣu*, in the Upaniṣads, as for instance in, 'There is no difference whatsoever in It' (Bṛ. IV. iv. 19; Ka. II. i. 11), 'The Lord on account of Māyā is perceived as manifold' (Bṛ. II. v. 19), 'This was but the Self in the beginning—the only entity' (Bṛ. I. iv. 17), 'In the beginning this was indeed Brahman, one only' (Bṛ. I. iv. 11), 'It is from a second entity that fear comes' (Bṛ. I. iv. 2), 'But there is not that second thing' (Bṛ. IV. iii. 23), 'But when to the knower of Brahman everything has become the Self' (Bṛ. IV. v. 15), and so on. (This is known) *vicakṣaṇaiḥ*, by those who are better acquainted with things, i.e. by the learned. This view is supported by the following Smṛti text of Vyāsa: '(This universe) is viewed (by the wise) as (unreal) like a crack on the ground that a rope appears to be in darkness, or as always (unstable) like bubbles created by rain, devoid of bliss and ceasing to exist after dissolution.'

न निरोधो न चोत्पत्तिर्न बद्धो न च साधकः।
न मुमुक्षुर्न वै मुक्त इत्येषा परमार्थता ॥३२॥

32. There is no dissolution, no origination, none in bondage, none striving or aspiring for salvation, and none liberated. This is the highest truth.

This verse is meant to sum up the purport of this chapter. If from the standpoint of the highest Reality, all duality is unreal, and the Self alone exists as the only Reality, then it amounts to this that all our dealings, conventional or scriptural, are surely matters of ignorance, and then there is *na nirodhaḥ*, no dissolution—*nirodha* being the same as *nirodhana*, stoppage—*utpattiḥ*, origination; *baddhaḥ*, one under bondage, a transmigrating individual soul; *sādhakaḥ*, one who strives for liberation; *mumukṣuḥ*, one who hankers after liberation; *muktaḥ*, one who is free from bondage. In the absence of origination and dissolution, bondage etc. do not exist. *Iti eṣā paramārthatā*, this is the highest Truth. How can there be absence of origination and dissolution? The answer is: Because of the absence of duality. The non-existence of duality is established by various Vedic texts such as, 'Because when there is duality, as it were' (Bṛ. II. iv. 14), '(He goes from death to death) who sees difference, as it were, in It' (Bṛ. IV. iv. 19; Ka. II. i. 10), 'All this is but the Self' (Ch. VII. xxv. 2), 'All this is but Brahman' (Nṛ. U. 7), 'One only, without a second' (Ch. VI. ii. 1), '(This Brāhmaṇa, . . .), and this all are this Self' (Bṛ. II. iv. 6; IV. v. 7). Origination or dissolution can belong only to a thing that has existence, and not to one that is non-existent like the horn of a hare. Nor can the non-dual have either birth or death. For it is a contradiction in terms to say that a thing is non-dual and yet has birth and death. And as for the empirical experience of Prāṇa etc., it has been already stated that it is all a superimposition on the Self, like a snake on a rope. Indeed, such a mental illusion[1] as the fancying of a rope for a snake does not either originate from or merge in the rope.[2] Nor does the rope-snake originate in the mind and merge there,[3] nor does it do so from both (the rope and the mind).[4] Similar is the case with duality which is equally a mental illusion, for duality is not perceived in a state of concentration or deep sleep. Therefore it is established that duality is a mere figment of the brain. And therefore it has been well said that since duality does not exist, the highest Truth consists in the non-existence of dissolution and the rest.

Objection: If such be the case, then the scriptures have for their objective only the proving of the non-existence of duality, not the proving of the existence of non-duality, the two objectives being contradictory. And as a result, one will be landed into nihilism, inasmuch as non-duality has no evidence in its support and duality is non-existent.

Answer: Not so, for why should you revive a point already dismissed with the statement that illusions, like that of a snake on a rope, cannot occur without a substratum?

To this the *objection* is raised thus: The rope that is

[1] A creation of ignorance subsisting in the mind.

[2] For the birth or death of an illusion is equally illusory. If these be objectively real, the snake should be perceived by all who see the rope.

[3] For if birth and death are only subjective, the snake should not be perceived outside.

[4] For it is not experienced as such.

supposed to be the substratum of the illusion of the snake is itself non-existent, and hence the analogy is irrelevant.

Answer: Not so, for even when the illusion disappears, the non-illusory substratum can continue to exist by the very fact of its being non-illusory.

Objection: The non-dual (substratum), too, is unreal like the snake fancied on a rope.

Answer: It cannot be so, for just as the rope constituting a factor in the illusion (of the snake) exists as an unimagined entity even before the knowledge of the non-existence of the snake, so also the non-dual (Self) eternally exists as a non-imagined entity. Besides, the being who is the agent of the imagination cannot be non-existent, since his existence has to be admitted antecedent to the rise of the illusion.[1]

Objection: But if the scriptures do not deal with the Self as such, how can they lead to a cessation of the awareness of duality?

Answer: That is no defect, for duality is superimposed on the Self through ignorance, just as a snake is on a rope.

Objection: How?

[1] The Self has to be assumed as the substratum of the illusory appearance of duality; It survives all illusions as the witness of their disappearance; and as a matter of course It precedes the illusion. Therefore there can be no question of nihilism even on the supposition that the Self is not presented positively by the Upaniṣads.

Answer: All such conceptions as, 'I am happy, miserable, ignorant, born, dead, worn out, embodied; I see; I am manifest and unmanifest, agent and enjoyer of fruits, related and unrelated, emaciated and old, these are mine,'—are superimposed on the Self. The Self permeates all these ideas, for It is invariably present in all of them, just as a rope is present in all its different (illusory) appearances as a snake, a line of water, etc. Such being the case, the knowledge of the nature of the substantive (Self) has not to be generated by scriptures, since It is self-established. The scriptures are meant for proving something that is not already known, for should they restate something that is already known they will lose their validity[1]. Since the Self is not established in Its own nature owing to the obstacle of such attributes as happiness that are superimposed by ignorance, and since remaining established in Its own reality is the highest goal, therefore the scriptures aim at removing from the Self the ideas of Its being happy and the rest by generating with regard to It the ideas of Its not being happy etc. through such texts as 'Not this, not this' (Bṛ. IV. iv. 22), 'Not gross' (Bṛ. III. viii. 8), etc. Unlike the real nature of the Self, the attributes of being unhappy etc., too, are not invariably present in consciousness simultaneously with such attributes as being happy etc.;[2] for if they were intrinsically

[1] Validity consisting in presenting something not known otherwise and not sublated later.

[2] If the attribute of 'being not happy' etc. are natural to the Self, why should they not accompany every perception of the latter? The answer is: The Self may reveal Itself, and yet the opposition

present, there can be no such distinguishing attribute as *being happy* etc. superimposed on It, just as there can be no coldness in fire possessed of the specific characteristic of heat. Therefore, it is in the attributeless Self that the distinct characteristics of *being happy* etc. are imagined. And as for the scriptural texts speaking of the absence of happiness etc. in the Self, it is proved that they are merely meant to remove the specific ideas of happiness etc. from It. And in support of this is the aphorism of those who are versed in the meaning of scriptures: 'The validity of the scriptures is derived from their negation of positive qualities from the Self.'[1]

The reason for the preceding verse is being adduced:

भावैरसद्भिरेवायमद्वयेन च कल्पितः ।
भावा अप्यद्वयेनैव तस्मादद्वयता शिवा ॥३३॥

33. This Self is imagined to be the unreal things and also to be non-dual; and these perceived things are also imagined on the non-dual Self. Therefore non-duality is auspicious.

---

between Its 'being not happy' etc. and Its empirical modes of 'being happy' etc. may not become patent owing to the influence of human ignorance.

[1] This is a quotation from Draviḍācārya. The idea is this: 'Though words may not have any positive meaning with regard to Brahman, the validity of the scripture is well established; for the words, that are associated with negation and are well known as denoting the absence of qualities, eliminate all duality from the Self.'

In (such illusions as) 'This is a snake', 'This is a stick', 'This is a streak of water', etc. the very thing called rope is imagined to be such unreal things as a snake, a streak of water, etc., and also as the one real thing—the rope; similarly, the Self is imagined to be such multifarious unreal things as Prāṇa etc. which do not exist. But this is not done from the standpoint of reality, for nothing can be pointed out by anybody unless the mind is active, nor can the Self have any movement. And things, perceivable to the unsteady mind alone, cannot be imagined to subsist in reality.[1] Therefore though the Self is ever of the same nature, It alone is imagined to be such unreal things as Prāṇa etc., and again as existing in Its own nature of non-duality and absolute Reality. It is supposed to be the substratum of everything, just as a rope is of the snake etc. And those perceived entities, too, viz Prāṇa and the rest, are imagined by virtue of the existence of the Self that is verily non-dual, for no illusion can be perceived that is without a substratum. Thus since non-duality is the substratum of all illusion, and since this non-duality is ever unchanging in its own nature, *advayatā*, non-duality; is *śivā*, auspicious, even in the state of illusion. But the illusions alone are evil, for they generate fear like that from the snake seen on a rope for instance. Non-duality is free from fear; hence that alone is auspicious.

[1] 'Diversity perceived on the motionless Self cannot be fancied to have real existence' is the interpretation according to Ānanda Giri, who takes 'motionless' as the meaning of '*pra-calita*, that in which motion is absent'.

नात्मभावेन नानेदं न स्वेनापि कथंचन ।
न पृथङ् नापृथक् किंचिदिति तत्त्वविदो विदुः ॥३४॥

34. This world, when ascertained from the standpoint of its essential nature, does not exist as different. Nor does it exist in its own right. Nor do phenomenal things exist as different or non-different (from one another or from the Self). This is what the knowers of Truth understood.

Why, again, is non-duality auspicious? Inauspiciousness is to be found where there is diversity or, in other words, where there is difference of one thing from another. For *idam*, this, the manifold phenomenal world, consisting of Prāṇa, etc.; when ascertained *ātmabhāvena*, from the standpoint of its essential nature, from the standpoint of supreme Reality; does not exist as *nānā*, multifarious, or as a different substance in this non-dual Self which is the absolute Reality, just as an illusory snake has no separate existence when it is found out with the help of a light to be identical with the rope. Besides, this world never exists *svena*, in its own nature, in the form of Prāṇa etc., verily because of its having been imagined like a snake on a rope. Similarly, the objects, called Prāṇa etc., are not distinct from each other in the sense that a buffalo exists as something different from a horse. Accordingly, just because of the unreality (of duality) there is nothing that can exist as non-separate from one another or from the supreme Self. The Brāhmaṇas, the knowers of the Self, *viduḥ* realized, the supreme Reality; *iti*, thus. Hence non-duality is auspicious, for it is free from the causes of evil. This is the purport.

The perfect realization, as described above, is being extolled:

वीतरागभयक्रोधैर्मुनिभिर्वेदपारगैः ।
निर्विकल्पो ह्ययं दृष्टः प्रपञ्चोपशमोऽद्वयः ॥३५॥

35. This Self that is beyond all imagination, free from the diversity of this phenomenal world, and non-dual, has been seen by the contemplative people, versed in the Vedas and unafflicted by desire, fear, and anger.

Munibhiḥ, by the constantly contemplative people, by the discriminating ones, from whom have been removed for ever attachment, fear, envy, anger, and all other faults; *vedapāragaiḥ*, by those who have understood the secrets of the Vedas, by the enlightened souls; by those who are devoted to the purport of the Upaniṣads; *dṛṣṭaḥ*, has been realized; *ayam*, this Self; which is *nirvikalpaḥ*, devoid of all imaginations; and which is *prapañcopaśamaḥ*: *prapañca* is the vast expanse of the variegated phenomenal world, and the Self in which there is the *upaśama*, total negation, of this, is the *prapañcopaśama*. And therefore It is *advayaḥ*, without a second. The idea is that the supreme Self is realizable only by the men of renunciation who are free from blemishes, who are learned, and who are devoted to the purport of the Upaniṣads, but not so by the logicians and others whose hearts are tainted by attachment etc. and whose philosophies are prejudiced by their own outlooks.

तस्मादेवं विदित्वैनमद्वैते योजयेत् स्मृतिम् ।
अद्वैतं समनुप्राप्य जडवल्लोकमाचरेत् ॥३६॥

36. Therefore, after knowing it thus, one should fix one's memory on (i.e. continuously think of) non-duality. Having attained the non-dual, one should behave in the world as though one were dull-witted.

Since non-duality is auspicious and free from fear by virtue of its being by nature devoid of all evil, therefore *viditvā enam*, having known it; *evam*, thus; *yojayet smṛtim*, one should fix one's memory; *advaite*, on non-duality; i.e. one should practise recollection for the realization of non-duality.[1] And having comprehended that non-duality etc., having realized directly and immediately that Self that is beyond hunger etc., birthless, and above all conventional dealings—after attaining the consciousness, 'I am the supreme Brahman'—*lokam ācaret*, one should behave in the world; *jaḍavat*, like a dull-witted man, that is to say, without advertising oneself as 'I am such and such'.

It is being stated as to what should be the code of conduct according to which he should behave in the world:

निस्तुतिर्निर्नमस्कारो निःस्वधाकार एव च ।
चलाचलनिकेतश्च यतिर्यादृच्छिको भवेत् ॥३७॥

37. The mendicant should have no appreciation or greetings (for others), and he should be free from

[1] Even after knowing the import of the Upaniṣads, there is need of continuously revolving in one's mind those ideas so that they may become firmly rooted.

rituals. He should have the body and soul as his support, and he should be dependent on circumstances.

Giving up all such activities as appreciation or greeting; that is to say, having given up all desire for external objects and having embraced the highest kind of formal renunciation, in accordance with the Vedic text, 'Knowing this very Self, the Brāhmaṇas renounce (. . . and lead a mendicant life)' (Bṛ. III. v. 1), and the Smṛti text, 'With their consciousness in That (Brahman), their Self identified with That, ever intent on That, with That for their supreme goal' (G. V. 17)—. *Cala*, the changing, is the body, since it gets transformed every moment; and *acala*, the unchanging, is the reality of the Self. Whenever perchance, impelled by the need of eating etc., one thinks of oneself as 'I' by forgetting the reality of the Self which is one's *niketa*, support, one's place of abode, and which is by nature unchanging like the sky, then the *cala*, changing body, becomes his *niketa*, support. The man of illumination who thus has the changing and the unchanging as his support, but not the man who has external objects as his support, is the *calācalaniketa*. And he *bhavet*, should be; *yādṛcchikaḥ*, dependent on circumstances; that is to say, he should merely depend on strips of cloth, coverings and food that come to him by chance for the maintenance of the body.

तत्त्वमाध्यात्मिकं दृष्ट्वा तत्त्वं दृष्ट्वा तु बाह्यतः ।
तत्त्वीभूतस्तदारामस्तत्त्वादप्रच्युतो भवेत् ॥३८॥

38. Examining the Reality in the context of the individual and in the external world, one should become identified with Reality, should have his delight in Reality, and should not deviate from Reality.

The external entities such as the earth, and the personal entities such as the body, are unreal like the snake imagined on a rope or like dream, magic, etc., in accordance with the Vedic text, 'All transformation has speech as its basis, and it is name only' (Ch. VI. iv. 1); and the Self is that which exists within and without, that is birthless, without cause and effect, without any inside or outside, full, all-pervasive like space, subtle, motionless, attributeless, partless, and actionless, as is indicated in the Vedic Text, 'That is Truth. That is the Self. That thou art' (Ch. VI. viii-xii). *Dṛṣṭvā*, having seen—the Reality in this way; *tattvībhūtaḥ*, (one should) become identified with Reality; *tadārāmaḥ*, (one should) have one's delight only in the Self, and not in anything external—like one lacking in realization, who accepts the mind as the Self, and thinks the Self to be changing in accordance with the changes of the mind, or at times accepts the body etc. to be the Self and thinks, 'I am now alienated from reality that is the Self'; and who at times when the mind becomes concentrated, thinks himself to be united with Reality and in peace under the belief, 'I am now identified with Reality'. The knower of the Self should not be like that, because the nature of the Self is ever the same, and because it is impossible for It to change Its nature; and one should be for ever *apracyutaḥ*, unwavering from Reality under the conviction, 'I am Brahman', that is to say, he should ever have the consciousness of the Reality that is the Self, in accordance with such Smṛti texts as, '(The enlightened man) views equally a dog or an outcast' (G. V. 18), '(He sees who sees the supreme Lord) existing equally in all beings' (G. XIII. 27), etc.

CHAPTER III

ADVAITA-PRAKARAṆA (ON NON-DUALITY)

In the course of determining the nature of *Om* (in Chap. I) it was stated as a mere proposition that the Self is the negation of the phenomenal world, and is auspicious and non-dual. It was further said that 'duality ceases to exist after realization' (*Kārikā*, I. 18). As to that, the non-existence of duality was established by the chapter 'On Unreality' with the help of such analogies as dream, magic, and a city in space, and through logic on the grounds of 'being perceived', 'having a beginning and an end', and so on. Should non-duality be admitted only on the authority of scripture (and tradition), or should it be accepted on logical grounds, too? In answer to this it is said that it can be known on logical grounds as well. The chapter 'On Non-duality' starts to show how this is possible. It was concluded in the preceding chapter that all diversity, comprising the worshipped, worship, and so on, is unreal and the absolute, non-dual Self is the highest Reality; for—

उपासनाश्रितो धर्मो जाते ब्रह्मणि वर्तते ।
प्रागुत्पत्तेरजं सर्वं तेनासौ कृपणः स्मृतः ॥१॥

1. The aspirant, betaking himself to the devotional exercises, subsists in the conditioned Brahman. All this was but the birthless Brahman before creation.

Hence such a man is considered pitiable (or narrow in his outlook).

Upāsanāśritaḥ is a worshipper who resorts to *upāsanā*, devotional exercises (like worship and meditation), as the means to his liberation, under the belief, 'I am a worshipper, and Brahman is to be adored by me. Though I now subsist *jāte brahmaṇi*, in the conditioned Brahman; I shall through my devotion to It, attain *ajam brahma*, the unconditioned Brahman, after the fall of my body. *Prāk utpatteḥ ajam sarvam*, before the creation all this, including myself, was but the birthless Brahman. Through my devotional exercises I shall regain that which I essentially was *prāk utpatteḥ*, before my birth, though, after being born, I now subsist *jāte brahmaṇi*, in the conditioned Brahman.' The *dharmaḥ*, aspirant; *upāsanāśritaḥ*, who betakes himself to such devotional exercises; since he is thus cognizant of the partial Brahman, *tena*, for that very reason; *asau*, that man; *smṛtaḥ*, is considered; *kṛpaṇaḥ*, pitiable, narrow (Bṛ. III. viii. 10), by those who have seen the eternal and birthless Brahman; this is the idea. And this is in accord with the following text of the Upaniṣad of the Talavakāra section: 'That which is not uttered by speech, that by which speech is revealed, know that alone to be Brahman, and not what people worship as an object' (Ke. I. 5).

अतो वक्ष्याम्यकार्पण्यमजाति समतां गतम् ।
यथा न जायते किंचिज्जायमानं समन्ततः ॥२॥

2. Hence I shall speak of that (Brahman) which

is free from limitation, has no birth, and is in a state of homogeneity; and listen how nothing whatsoever is born in any way, though it seems to be born.

Since on account of one's failure to attain the birthless Self existing within and without, one becomes pitiable by thinking oneself through ignorance to be unworthy, and since on that account one comes to believe, 'I am born, I subsist in the conditioned Brahman, and having recourse to Its worship I shall attain (the unconditioned) Brahman', *ataḥ*, therefore; *vakṣyāmi*, I shall relate; *akārpaṇyam*, freedom from misery, limitlessness, the birthless Brahman; for that indeed is a source of limitation, 'where one sees another, hears another, knows another. That is limited, mortal, and unreal' (cf. Ch. VII. xxiv. 1), as is asserted in such Vedic texts as, 'All transformation has speech as its basis, and it is name only' (Ch. VI. iv. 1). Opposed to this is That which has no limitation, which is within and without and is the birthless Brahman, called the Infinite, on realizing which there is cessation of all misery caused by ignorance. I shall speak of that freedom from limits. This is the purport. That thing is *ajāti*, birthless; *samatām gatam*, established in a state of total homogeneity. Why? Since It has no inequality of parts. Anything that is composite is said to evolve when its parts undergo loss of balance. But since this thing is partless, It is established in homogeneity, and hence It does not evolve through any change in any part. Therefore, It is birthless and free from misery. Hear *yathā*, how; *samantataḥ*, in all respects; *kiṁcit*, anything, small though it be; *na jāyate*, is not born; though *jāyamānam*, it may (seem to) be born, like a snake from a rope, in consequence of perception under ignorance. Hear how It is not born—how Brahman remains unborn in every way. This is the idea.

The promise was, 'I shall speak of Brahman which has no birth and which is free from limitation.' Now it is said, 'I shall adduce the reason and the analogy for proving this':

आत्मा ह्याकाशवज्जीवैर्घटाकाशैरिवोदितः ।
घटादिवच्च संघातैर्जातावेतन्निदर्शनम् ॥३॥

3. Since the Self is referred to as existing in the form of individual souls in the same way as space exists in the form of spaces confined within jars, and since the Self exists in the form of the composite things just as space exists as jars etc., therefore in the matter of birth this is the illustration.

Hi, since; *ātmā*, the (supreme) Self; is subtle, partless, and all-pervasive *ākāśavat*, like space—since that very supreme Self that is comparable to space; *uditaḥ*, is referred to; *jīvaiḥ*, as existing in the form of individual souls, the individual knowers of the bodies etc.; *iva*, in the same way; *ākāśavat ghaṭākāśaiḥ*, as space is referred to as existing in the form of spaces circumscribed by jars. Or the explanation is: As space (*uditaḥ*) comes to exist in the form of spaces within the jars, so also has the supreme Self come to exist as the individual souls. The idea implied is that the emergence of individual souls from the supreme Self, that is heard of in the Upaniṣads, is comparable to the emergence of the spaces in the jars from the supreme space; but this is not so in any real sense of the term. Just as from that very space evolve composite things like jars etc., so also from the supreme Self, which is comparable to space, emerge the composite things like the earth etc., as well as the bodies and senses that constitute the individual, all of them taking birth through imagination like a snake on a rope. This fact is stated in *ghaṭādivat ca*, and like a jar etc.; It is evolved *saṁghātaiḥ*, in the form of composite things. When with a view to make the fact understood by people of poor intellect, the birth of creatures etc. from the Self is referred to by the Vedas, then *jātau*, with regard to birth, when that is taken for granted; *etat nidarśanam*, this is the illustration, as it has been cited in the analogy of space etc.

घटादिषु प्रलीनेषु घटाकाशादयो यथा ।
आकाशे संप्रलीयन्ते तद्वज्जीवा इहात्मनि ॥४॥

4. Just as the space confined within the jars etc. merge completely on the disintegration of the jars etc., so do the individual souls merge here in this Self.

Just as the spaces within a jar etc. emerge into being with the creation of the jar etc., or just as the spaces within the jar etc., disappear with the disintegration of the jar etc., similarly, the individual souls emerge into being along with the creation of the aggregates of bodies etc., and they merge here in the Self on the disintegration of those aggregates. But this is not so from their own standpoint.

The next verse is by way of an answer to those dualists who argue, 'If there be but one Self in all the bodies, then when one of the souls undergoes birth or death or enjoys happiness etc., all souls should share in these; besides there will be a confusion of actions and their results.'

यथैकस्मिन् घटाकाशे रजोधूमादिभिर्युते।
न सर्वे संप्रयुज्यन्ते तद्वज्जीवाः सुखादिभिः ॥५॥

5. Just as all the spaces confined within the various jars are not darkened when one of the spaces thus confined becomes contaminated by dust, smoke, etc., so also is the case with all the individuals in the matter of being affected by happiness etc.

Yathā, just as; *ekasmin ghaṭākāśe rajodhūmādibhiḥ yute*, when one of the spaces confined in a jar is polluted by dust, smoke, etc.; *na*, not; *sarve*, all the spaces, confined within the jars etc., are defiled by that dust or smoke etc.; *tadvat*, just like that; *jīvāḥ*, creatures; are not affected *sukhādibhiḥ*, by happiness etc.

Objection: Is not the Self but one?

Answer: Quite so. Did you not hear that there is but one Self which like space inhabits all the aggregates (of body and senses)?

Objection: If the Self be one, It will experience happiness and sorrow everywhere.

Answer: This objection cannot be raised by the Sāṁkhyas. For a follower of the Sāṁkhya philosophy cannot posit happiness, sorrow, etc. in the soul, inasmuch as he declares that joy, misery, etc. inhere in the intellect. Moreover, there is no valid ground for imagining that the Self, which is Consciousness by nature, has any multiplicity.

Objection: In the absence of multiplicity, the (Sāṁkhya) theory that the Pradhāna (i.e. Primordial Nature) acts for others (viz the Puruṣas, the conscious souls) has no leg to stand on.

Answer: No, since whatever is accomplished by the Pradhāna cannot get inseparably connected with the Self. If it were a fact that any result in the form of either bondage or freedom brought about by Pradhāna inhered in the souls separately, then the supposition of a single Self would run counter to the (Sāṁkhya) theory that the Pradhāna acts for others, and therefore it would be logical to assume a multiplicity of souls. But as a matter of fact, it is not admitted by the Sāṁkhyas that any result, be it bondage or freedom, which is accomplished by the Pradhāna, inheres in the soul; on the contrary, they hold that the souls are attributeless and are pure consciousness. Hence the theory that the Pradhāna acts for others, derives its validity from the mere presence of the Self, and not from Its multiplicity. Therefore the fact that the Pradhāna acts for others, cannot be a logical ground for inferring the existence of many souls. And the Sāṁkhyas have no other proof to validate their theory that each soul is different from all others. If it be held that the Pradhāna itself undergoes bondage or liberation by virtue of this mere presence of the supreme One (viz God), and that God becomes an occasion for the activity of the Pradhāna by the mere fact of His existence—which is the same as pure Consciousness—and not on account of any specific quality, then the assumption of a multiplicity of souls and the rejection of the meaning of the Vedas are the results of mere stupidity.[1]

As for the view of the Vaiśeṣikas and others who assert that desire and the rest inhere in the soul, that, too, is untenable; for the impressions (of past experiences) that generate memory cannot remain inseparably located in the Self that has no location. And since (according to them) memory arises from a contact of the soul with the mind, there can be no fixed rule regarding the rise of memory; or there will be the possibility of the rise of all kinds of memory simultaneously. Moreover, the souls that are devoid of touch etc. and belong to a different category cannot logically come into contact with mind etc. Furthermore, it is not a fact, though these others believe in it, that qualities like colour or such categories as action, genus, species, or inherence exist independently of the substances. If they were absolutely different from substances, and if desire etc. were so from the soul, those qualities etc. would not have any reasonable relation with substance, (nor would desire etc. have any relation with the soul).

[1] This refutes the view of those Sāṁkhyas who believe in one God as well as in a multiplicity of souls.

Objection: It involves no contradiction to say that categories which become associated from their very birth can have the relationship of inherence.

Answer: Not so; since the eternal Self exists before the ephemeral moods like desire, no theory of congenital inherence can be logically advanced. If on the contrary, desire and the rest are supposed to have an inseparable relation with the soul from their very birth, then there arises the possibility of their becoming as everlasting as the quality of vastness that the soul possesses (even according to the Vaiśeṣikas). And that is not a desirable position, for that will lead to the conclusion that the soul has no freedom from the bondage (of desire etc). Besides, if the relationship of inherence be different from a substance, then one has to posit another relationship for its being connected with the substance, just as much as such a relationship (viz conjunction) is assumed in the case of substance and quality (by Vaiśeṣikas).

Objection: Inherence being verily an eternal, inseparable connection, there is no need of positing another relationship to connect it (with a substance).

Answer: In that case, since entities that are connected through the relation of inherence remain eternally joined, there can be no possibility of their being separate. Alternatively, if the substances and the rest be absolutely disparate, then just as things possessing and not possessing the attribute of touch cannot come in contact, so also those substances etc. cannot become related (with such categories as relation, qualities, etc.) by way of possession that is implied by the sixth case.[1] Besides, if the Self is possessed of such qualities as desire etc. that are subject to increase and decrease, It will be open to the charge of being impermanent like the bodies and the fruits of actions. And the other two faults of Its being possessed of parts and being subject to mutation, just like the bodies etc., will be unavoidable. On the other hand, if on the analogy of the sky, appearing to be blackened by dust and smoke attributed to it through ignorance, it is supposed that the Self appears to be possessed of the defects of happiness and sorrow generated by such limiting adjuncts as the intellect that are superimposed on It through ignorance, there remains no illogicality in Its possessing bondage, freedom etc. in an empirical sense. For all schools of thought, while admitting the empirical reality as originating from ignorance, deny its absolute reality. Therefore the imagination of the multiplicity of souls that the logician resorts to is quite uncalled for.

It is being shown how, through ignorance, there can be the possibility, in the same Self, of that same variety of actions which becomes possible on the assumption of a multiplicity of souls:

रूपकार्यसमाख्याश्च भिद्यन्ते तत्र तत्र वै ।
आकाशस्य न भेदोऽस्ति तद्वज्जीवेषु निर्णयः ॥६॥

[1] We cannot say for instance, 'This thing is related to that colour through inherence', which in ordinary parlance is expressed by saying, 'This thing has that colour.'

6. Though forms, actions, and names differ in respect of the difference (in the spaces created by jars etc.), yet there is no multiplicity in space. So also is the definite conclusion with regard to the individual beings.

As in the same space there is a (supposed) difference of dimension such as smallness and bigness in respect of the spaces enclosed by a jar, a water bowl, a house, etc., so also there is a difference of functions such as fetching or holding water, sleeping, etc., and of names such as the space in a jar, the space in a water bowl, the space in a house, etc., which are all created by those jar etc.; but all these differences are not surely real that are implied in conventional dealings involving dimensions etc. created in space; in reality *ākāśasya na bhedaḥ asti*, space has no difference, nor can there be any empirical dealing based on the multiplicity of space unless there be the instrumentality of the limiting adjuncts. Just as it is the case here, so also *jīveṣu*, with regard to the souls, which are created as individual beings by the conditioning factors of the bodies and are comparable to spaces enclosed by jars; this *nirṇayaḥ*, definite conclusion, has been arrived at by the wise after examination. This is the purport.

नाकाशस्य घटाकाशो विकारावयवौ यथा ।
नैवात्मनः सदा जीवो विकारावयवौ तथा ॥७॥

7. As the space within a jar is neither a transformation nor a part of space (as such), so an indi-

vidual being is never a transformation nor a part of the supreme Self.

Objection: The experience of difference so far as forms, actions, etc. are concerned with regard to those spaces in a jar etc. follows a real pattern.

Answer: This does not accord with fact, since *ghaṭā-kāśaḥ*, the space within a jar; *na vikāraḥ*, is not a transformation of the real space, in the sense that a piece of gold ornament is of gold, or foam, bubbles, ice, etc. are of water; nor is it *avayavaḥ*, a part, as for instance the branches etc. are of a tree. *Yathā*, as; the space in a jar is not a transformation of space in that sense; *tathā*, similarly, just as shown in the illustration; *jīvaḥ*, an individual being, that is comparable to the space within a jar; is *na sadā*, never; either a transformation or even a part *ātmanaḥ*, of the supreme Self, that is the highest Reality and is comparable to the infinite space. Therefore the dealings, based on the multiplicity of the Self, must certainly be false. This is the idea.

Inasmuch as the experience of birth, death, etc. follows as a consequence of the differentiation among individuals created by the limiting adjuncts constituted by the bodies, just as the experience of the forms, actions, etc. are the results of the ideas of difference entertained with regard to the spaces within a jar etc., therefore the association of the soul with such impurities as suffering and consequences of actions is caused by that alone, but not in any real sense. With a view to establishing this fact with the help of an illustration the text goes on:

यथा भवति बालानां गगनं मलिनं मलैः ।
तथा भवत्यबुद्धानामात्माऽपि मलिनो मलैः ॥८॥

8. Just as the sky becomes blackened by dust etc. to the ignorant, so also the Self becomes tarnished by impurities to the unwise.

Yathā, as, in common experience; *gaganam*, the sky; *bhavati*, becomes; *malinam*, blackened; by cloud, dust, smoke, and such other *malaiḥ*, impurities; *bālānām*, to the non-discriminating people; but to the truly discriminating people, the sky is not blackened; *tathā*, so also; *abuddhānām*, to the unwise, to those only who cannot distinguish the indwelling Self—but not to those who can distinguish the Self; *ātmā*, even the supreme Self, the knower and the innermost; *bhavati*, becomes; *malinaḥ*, tainted; *malaiḥ*, with impurities—the impurities of mental defects and results of actions. For a desert does not become possessed of water, foam, wave, etc. just because a thirsty creature falsely attributes these to it. Similarly, the Self is not blemished by the impurities of suffering etc. attributed to It by the ignorant. This is the idea.

The same idea is being elaborated again:

मरणे संभवे चैव गत्यागमनयोरपि ।
स्थितौ सर्वशरीरेषु आकाशेनाविलक्षणः ॥९॥

9. The Self is not dissimilar to space in the matter of Its death and birth, as well as Its going and coming, and existence in all the bodies.

The idea implied is that one should realize that in the matter of birth, death, etc., the Self in all the bodies is quite on a par with space in its relation to the space confined in a jar, so far as origination, destruction, coming, going, and motionlessness are concerned.

संघाताः स्वप्नवत्सर्वे आत्ममायाविसर्जिताः ।
आधिक्ये सर्वसाम्ये वा नोपपत्तिर्हि विद्यते ॥१०॥

10. The aggregates (of bodies and senses) are all projected like dream by the Māyā of the Self. Be it a question of superiority or equality of all, there is no logical ground to prove their existence.

Saṁghātāḥ, the aggregates, of bodies etc., that are analogous to the jars etc., are like the bodies etc. seen in a dream and like those conjured up by a magician; and are *ātma-māyā-visarjitāḥ*, projected, conjured up, by the Māyā, ignorance, of the Self; the idea is that they do not exist in reality. Though there may be *ādhikya*, superiority, of the aggregates of the bodies and senses of the gods and others in comparison with those of the beasts and others; or there may be *sāmya*, equality of all; still *hi*, since; there exists *na upapattiḥ*, no valid ground, no possibility, for them—there is no reason establishing the existence of these things; therefore they are created by ignorance alone—they do not exist in reality. This is the meaning.

(Upaniṣadic) texts that go to establish the fact that the reality of the non-dual Self is proved on the evidence of the Vedas, are now being referred to:

रसादयो हि ये कोशा व्याख्यातास्तैत्तिरीयके ।
तेषामात्मा परो जीवः खं यथा संप्रकाशितः ॥११॥

11. It has been amply elucidated (by us) on the analogy of space, that the individual living being that conforms to the soul of the sheaths, counting from that constituted by the essence of food, which have been fully dealt with in the Taittirīya Upaniṣad, is none other than the supreme Self.

Rasādayaḥ, the essence of food etc., that is to say, the layers of covering — (so called) since the preceding ones are more and more external in relation to the succeeding ones — constituted by the essence of food, the vital force, etc. which are comparable to the sheaths of swords; have been *vyākhyātāḥ*, fully dealt with; *taittirīyake*, in a part of the Upaniṣad of the Taittirīyaka branch (Tai. II. i-vi). That which is *ātmā*, the soul, the inmost entity; *teṣām*, of them, of all the sheaths; because of which (soul) all the five sheaths come to have existence; is *jīvaḥ*, the living being, since it is the source of animation of all. It is being said as to what it is. It is *paraḥ*, the supreme Self (Brahman) Itself, that was introduced earlier in the text, 'Brahman is Truth, Knowledge, and Infinite' (Tai. II. i) — the Self from which, it was stated that, through the Māyā of the Self, emerged like dream or magic (*Kārikā*, III. 10) (first) space etc. and then the composite things called the sheaths counting from the one composed of the essence of food (Tai. II. i). That very Self *saṁprakāśitaḥ*, has been held forth by us as analogous to space, in the verses beginning with

'Since the Self is referred to as existing in the form of individual souls in the same way as space . . .' (*Kārikā*, III. 3). The idea implied is that, unlike the self imagined by the logicians, the Self is not to be established by the mere means of the human intellect.

द्वयोर्द्वयोर्मधुज्ञाने परं ब्रह्म प्रकाशितम्।
पृथिव्यामुदरे चैव यथाऽऽकाशः प्रकाशितः ॥१२॥

12. As it is demonstrated that space in the earth and the stomach is but the same, similarly in the Madhu-Brāhmaṇa the supreme Brahman is revealed as the same with reference to the different dual contexts.

Moreover, *prakāśitam*, it has been revealed; *dvayoḥ dvayoḥ*, with reference to the different dual contexts—the superhuman and the corporeal—that the 'shining, immortal being' dwelling inside the earth etc. as the knower, is but Brahman, the supreme Self, which is everything (Bṛ. II. v. 1-14). Where (has this been revealed)? That is being stated: The word *madhujñāna* is used in the sense of that from which is known *madhu*, nectar, called the knowledge of Brahman—it being ambrosial since it leads to blissfulness; so it means the (chapter called) Madhu-Brāhmaṇa (of the Bṛhadāraṇyaka Upaniṣad). In that Madhu-Brāhmaṇa. Like what? *Yathā*, as, in the world; the same *ākāśaḥ*, space; is *prakāśitaḥ*, demonstrated to exist, through inference; *pṛthivyām udare ca eva*, in the earth and the stomach; similar is the case here. This is the purport.

जीवात्मनोरनन्यत्वमभेदेन प्रशस्यते ।
नानात्वं निन्द्यते यच्च तदेवं हि समञ्जसम् ॥१३॥

13. The fact that the non-difference of the individual and the supreme Self is extolled by a statement of their identity, and the fact that diversity is condemned, become easy of comprehension from this point of view alone.

The fact that *ananyatvam jīvātmanaḥ*, the non-difference of the individual soul and the supreme Self, ascertained through reasoning and the Vedas; is *praśasyate*, praised, by the scriptures and Vyāsa and others; *abhedena*, by a reference to (the result consisting in) the identity (of the individual and the supreme Self);[1] and the fact that the perception of multiplicity, which is common and natural to all beings and is a view formulated by the sophists standing outside the pale of scriptural import, *nindyate*, is condemned, by the knowers of Brahman as well by such and other texts as, 'But there is not that second' (Bṛ. IV. iii. 23), 'It is from a second entity that fear comes' (Bṛ. I. iv. 2), 'For, whenever the aspirant creates the slightest difference in It, he is smitten with fear' (Tai. II. vii. 1), '. . . and this all are this Self' (Bṛ. II. iv. 6; IV. v. 7), 'He who perceives multiplicity here, as it were, goes from death to death' (Ka. II. i. 10); *tat yat*, all that, which has been said (thus); *samañjasam*, becomes easy of comprehension, that is to say, becomes logical; *evam hi*, from this point of view alone; but the per-

[1] 'Anyone who knows that supreme Brahman becomes Brahman indeed' (Mu. III. ii. 9).

verted views, cooked up by the logicians, are not easy of comprehension; that is to say, they do not tally with facts when probed into.

जीवात्मनोः पृथक्त्वं यत्प्रागुत्पत्तेः प्रकीर्तितम् ।
भविष्यद्वृत्त्या गौणं तन्मुख्यत्वं हि न युज्यते ॥१४॥

14. The separateness of the individual and the supreme Self that has been declared (in the Vedic texts) earlier than (the talk of)creation (in the Upaniṣads), is only in a secondary sense that keeps in view a future result (viz unity); for such separateness is out of place in its primary sense.

Objection: Since *prāk utpatteḥ*, earlier even than the Upaniṣadic texts dealing with creation; *pṛthaktvam jīvātmanoḥ*, the separateness of the individual and the supreme Self; *prakīrtitam*, has been declared; by the Vedas, in the portion dealing with rites and duties, in various ways in conformity with the variety of desires (of individuals), in such words as, 'desirous of this', 'desirous of that', and the supreme Self, too, has been declared in such *mantra* texts as, 'He held the earth as well as this heaven' (Ṛ. X. cxxi. 1), therefore, in case of a contradiction between the sentences of the portions on knowledge (i.e. Upaniṣads) and rites (i.e. Saṁhitā and Brāhmaṇa), why should unity alone, standing out as the purport of the portion on knowledge, be upheld as the reasonable one?

To this the *answer* is: *Tat pṛthaktvam*, that separateness; is not the highest Truth; *yat*, which; is *prakīrtitam*, declared; *prāk*, earlier in the portion on rites, before the Upaniṣadic texts dealing with creation occur, to wit, 'That from which all these beings take birth' (Tai. III. i), 'As from a fire tiny sparks fly' (Bṛ. II. i. 20), 'From that Brahman indeed, which is this Self, space was created' (Tai. II. i. 1), 'That (Self) saw (i.e. deliberated)' (Ch. VI. ii. 3), 'That (Self) created fire' (ibid), etc. What is it then? It is *gauṇam*, secondary, like the separateness of the infinite space and the space within a jar. And this statement is made by keeping in view the future result, as in the sentence, 'He cooks food.'[1] For the texts speaking of difference can never reasonably uphold it in any literal sense, inasmuch as the texts dealing with the multiplicity of the Self only reiterate the diverse experiences of beings still under natural ignorance. And here in the Upaniṣads, too, in the texts speaking of creation, dissolution, etc., the one thing sought to be established is the unity of the individual and the supreme Self, as is known from such texts as, 'That thou art' (Ch. VI. viii-xvi), '(While he who worships another god thinking), "He is one, and I am another" does not know' (Bṛ. I. iv. 10), etc. Therefore the reiteration of the perception of multiplicity is made by the Vedas in this world in a secondary sense only, placing their reliance on the future demonstration of unity that is left over as a task to be accomplished in the Upaniṣads at a later stage. Or the explanation is this: The declaration of unity has been made in, 'One only, without a second' (Ch. VI. ii. 2), earlier than that of creation introduced

[1] Where food stands for the ultimate form that the things being cooked will assume.

in such texts as, 'That (Self) deliberated', 'That created fire' (Ch. VI. ii. 2-3) etc. And that, again, will culminate in unity in the text, 'That is truth, That is the Self, and That thou art' (Ch. VI. viii-xvi). Therefore the separateness of the individual and the supreme Self that is met with (in the Upaniṣads) anywhere in any sentence must be taken in a secondary sense, as in the sentence, 'He cooks food', for the thing kept in view here is the unity that will be established in future.

Objection: Even though everything be birthless and one without a second before creation, still after creation all these surely have got birth, and individuals, too, are different.

Answer: This is not so, for the Vedic texts dealing with creation have a different object in view. This objection was refuted earlier also by saying that, just like dream, the aggregates are created by the Māyā of the Self, and that birth, difference, etc. of individuals are analogous to birth, difference, etc. of the spaces within jars (*Kārikā*, III. 9-10). (Since falsity of these have already been dealt with) therefore, taking that very reason for granted, some Vedic texts dealing with creation are being adduced here, from amongst the texts dealing with creation, difference, etc., with a view to showing that they are meant for establishing the oneness of the Self and the individual beings.

मृल्लोहविस्फुलिङ्गाद्यैः सृष्टिर्या चोदिताऽन्यथा ।
उपायः सोऽवताराय नास्ति भेदः कथंचन ॥१५॥

15. The creation that has been multifariously set forth with the help of the examples of earth, gold, sparks, etc., is merely by way of generating the idea (of oneness); but there is no multiplicity in any way.

Sṛṣṭiḥ, the creation; *yā*, which; *coditā*, has been expounded, revealed; *anyathā*, in different ways; *mṛt-loha-visphuliṅga-ādyaiḥ*, with the help of such illustrations as earth, gold, sparks, etc.;[1] *saḥ*, that, all that process of creation; is a *upāyaḥ*, means; *avatārāya*, for engendering, in us the idea of the oneness of the individual and the supreme Self. It is just like the story of the organs of speech etc. becoming smitten with sin by the devils, that is woven round a conversation with Prāṇa, where the intention is to generate the idea of pre-eminence of Prāṇa (Ch. I. ii; Bṛ. I. iii., VI. i; Pr. II).

Objection: That, too, is unacceptable.[2]

Answer: No, since the conversations of Prāṇa etc. are related divergently in the different branches of the Vedas. If the colloquies were really true, we should have met with a uniform pattern in all the branches, and not with heterogeneous contradictory presentations. But, as a matter of fact, divergence is met with. Therefore the Vedic texts setting forth the interlogues are not to be taken literally. So also are to be understood the sentences dealing with creation.

Objection: Since the cycles of creation differ, the

[1] Ch. VI. i. 4-6; Mu. II. i. 1.

[2] The anecdotes of Prāṇa are real.

Vedic texts dealing with the interlogues, as well as with creation, are divergent with relation to the respective cycles.

Answer: Not so, since they serve no useful purpose apart from generating the ideas already mentioned. Not that any other purpose can be imagined for the Vedic texts speaking of colloquies and creation.

Objection: They are meant for meditation with a view to attaining self-identification.

Answer: Not so, for it cannot be a desirable end to be identified with quarrel, creation, or dissolution. Therefore the texts expressing creation etc. are meant simply for generating the idea of the oneness of the Self, and they cannot be fancied to bear other interpretations. Therefore *na asti*, there is not; any *bhedaḥ*, multiplicity, caused by creation etc; *kathaṁcana*, in any way.

Objection: If in accordance with such Vedic texts as, 'One only, without a second' (Ch. VI. ii. 2), the supreme Self, that is by nature ever pure, intelligent, and free, be the only reality in the highest sense and all else be unreal, then why are there such instructions on meditations in the Vedic texts as, 'The Self, my dear, should be realized'[1] (Bṛ. II. iv. 5), 'The Self that is devoid of sin . . . (is to be sought for)', (Ch. VIII. vii. 1), 'He should shape his conviction' (Ch. III. xiv. 1), 'The Self alone is to be meditated upon' (Bṛ.

[1] The remaining portion is: 'heard of, deliberated on, and meditated on'.

I. iv. 7), etc.; and why are the rites like Agnihotra enjoined?

Answer: Hear the reason for this:

आश्रमास्त्रिविधा हीनमध्यमोत्कृष्टदृष्टयः ।
उपासनोपदिष्टेयं तदर्थमनुकम्पया ॥१६॥

16. There are three stages of life—inferior, intermediate, and superior. This meditation is enjoined for them out of compassion.

The word *āśramāḥ* meaning stages of life, indicates the people belonging to them—the people competent for scriptural duties, as well as the people of different castes following the righteous path—for the word is used in a suggestive sense. They are *trividhāḥ*, of three kinds. How? *Hīna-madhyama-utkṛṣṭa-dṛṣṭayaḥ*, people possessing inferior, medium, and superior power of vision; that is to say, they are endued with dull, medium, and fine mental calibre. *Iyam upāsanā*, this meditation, as well as rites; *upadiṣṭā*, has been instructed; *tadartham*, for them, for the sake of people of dull and medium intellect who are affiliated to the stages of life etc., and not for the people of superior intellect having the conviction that the Self is but one without a second. (This is done) by the kind Vedas, *anukampayā*, out of compassion, as to how people, by treading the path of righteousness, may attain this superior vision of unity from such Vedic texts as, 'That which is not thought of by the mind, that by which, they say, the mind is encompassed, know that to be

Brahman, and not this that people worship as an object' (Ke. I. 6), 'That thou art' (Ch. VI. vii-xvi), 'The Self indeed is all this' (Ch. VII. xxv. 2), etc.

The perfect knowledge consists in the realization of the non-dual Self, since this is established by scriptures and logic, whereas any other view is false, it being outside the pale of these. A further reason that the theories of the dualists are false is that they are based on such defects as likes and dislikes. How?

स्वसिद्धान्तव्यवस्थासु द्वैतिनो निश्चिता दृढम् ।
परस्परं विरुध्यन्ते तैरयं न विरुध्यते ॥१७॥

17. The dualists, confirmed believers in the methodologies establishing their own conclusions, are at loggerheads with one another. But this (non-dual) view has no conflict with them.

Dvaitinaḥ, the dualists—who follow the views of Kapila, Kaṇāda, Buddha, Arhat,[1] and others; *niścitāḥ*, are firmly rooted; *svasiddhānta-vyavasthāsu*, in the methodologies leading to their own conclusions. Thinking, 'The supreme Reality is this alone, and not any other', they remain affiliated to those points of view; and finding anyone opposed to them, they become hateful of him. Thus being swayed by likes and dislikes, consequent on the adherence to their own conclusions, *parasparam virudhyante*, they stand arrayed against one another. As one is not at conflict with

[1] Viz the Sāṁkhyas, Nyāya-Vaiśeṣikas, Buddhists, and Jainas.

one's own hands and feet, so also, just because of non-difference from all, *ayam*, this, this Vedic view of ours consisting in seeing the same Self in everyone; *na virudhyate*, is not opposed; *taiḥ*, to them, who are mutually at conflict. Thus the idea sought to be conveyed is that the perfect view consists in realizing the Self as one, for this is not subject to the drawbacks of love and hatred.

It is being pointed out why this view does not conflict with theirs:

अद्वैतं परमार्थो हि द्वैतं तद्भेद उच्यते।
तेषामुभयथा द्वैतं तेनायं न विरुध्यते॥१८॥

18. Non-duality is the highest Reality, since duality is said to be a product of it. But for them there is duality either way. Therefore this view (of ours) does not clash (with theirs).

Advaitam paramārthaḥ, non-duality is the highest Reality; *hi*, since; *dvaitam*, duality, heterogeneity; is *tad-bhedaḥ*, a differentiation, that is to say, a product, of that non-duality, in accordance with the Vedic texts, '(In the beginning there was Existence alone)—One only, without a second. . . . It created fire' (Ch. VI. ii. 2-3), and in accordance with reason also; for duality ceases to exist in *samādhi* (God-absorption), unconsciousness, and deep sleep, when one's mind ceases to act. Therefore duality is called a product of non-duality. But *teṣām*, for those dualists; there is nothing but *dvaitam*, duality; *ubhayathā*, from either point of view, from the standpoints of both (absolute) Reality and (empirical) reality. Though those deluded persons have a dualist outlook and we the undeluded ones have a non-dualist outlook in confromity with the Vedic texts, 'The Lord, on account of Māyā, is perceived as many' (Bṛ. II. v. 19), 'But there is not that second thing (separate from It which It can see)' (Bṛ. IV. iii. 23); yet *tena*, because of this reason (because of the falsity of dualism); *ayam*, this our point of view; *na virudhyate*, does not clash, with theirs. This point can be illustrated thus: A man sitting astride an elephant in rut does not goad his animal against a madman standing on the ground and challenging him by saying, 'I am also seated on an elephant in opposition; drive your animal against me', just because he has no inimical feelings towards the latter. Thus, since in reality, the knower of Brahman is the very Self of the dualists, *tena*, hence, because of this reason; *ayam*, this, this outlook of ours; *na virudhyate*, does not clash, with them.

When it is asserted that duality is derived from non-duality, someone may entertain the doubt that on that ground duality, too, is real in the highest sense. Therefore it is said:

मायया भिद्यते ह्येतन्नान्यथाऽजं कथञ्चन ।
तत्त्वतो भिद्यमाने हि मर्त्यताममृतं व्रजेत् ॥१९॥

19. This birthless (Self) becomes differentiated verily through Māyā, and it does so in no other way

than this. For should It become multiple in reality, the immortal will undergo mortality.

The fact that non-duality which is the highest Reality, *bhidyate*, differentiates; *hi*, verily; *māyayā*, through Māyā, is like the moon seen as many by a man with diseased eyes, or like a rope appearing diversely as a snake, a line of water, etc; but it is not so in reality, for the Self has no parts. A composite thing can get transformed through a change in its components, as earth gets modified into jars etc. Therefore the idea conveyed is that the partless *ajam*, birthless (Self); differentiates, *na kathañcana*, in no way whatsoever; *anyathā*, other than this. *Hi*, for; *tattvataḥ bhidyamāne*, should (It) become multiformed in reality; that which is naturally *amṛtam*, immortal; *ajam*, birthless; and non-dual; *vrajet martyatām*, will undergo mortality, like fire becoming cold. And this reversal of one's own nature is repugnant, since it is opposed to all valid evidence. The birthless, undecaying Reality that is the Self, becomes multiple through Māyā alone and not in reality. Therefore duality is not the highest Truth.

अजातस्यैव भावस्य जातिमिच्छन्ति वादिनः ।
अजातो ह्यमृतो भावो मर्त्यतां कथमेष्यति ॥२०॥

20. The talkers vouch indeed for the birth of that very unborn, positive entity. But how can a positive entity that is unborn and immortal undergo mortality?

But those, again, who talk of Brahman, who are

vādinaḥ, garrulous interpreters of the Upaniṣads; *icchanti*, they vouch for; the *jātim*, birth, in a real sense; *ajātasya eva*, of the One which is verily birthless, which is by nature immortal, the Reality that is the Self. If the Self be born as they hold, It *eṣyati martyatām*, will undergo mortality, for a certainty. But that Self, being by nature a *bhāvaḥ*, positive entity; that is *ajātaḥ*, unborn; and *amṛtaḥ*, deathless; *katham*, how; can It undergo mortality? The idea is that It will in no way reverse Its nature to embrace mortality (which individuals are subject to).

न भवत्यमृतं मर्त्यं न मर्त्यममृतं तथा ।
प्रकृतेरन्यथाभावो न कथञ्चिद्भविष्यति ॥२१॥

21. The immortal cannot become mortal. Similarly the mortal cannot become immortal. The mutation of one's nature will take place in no way whatsoever.

Because, in this world, the *amṛtam*, immortal; *na bhavati*, does not become; *martyam*, mortal; and similarly, the mortal also does not become immortal; therefore, *anyathābhāvaḥ prakṛteḥ*, the mutation of one's nature, becoming anything other than what one is; *na katham cit bhaviṣyati*, will not take place in any way whatsoever, just as fire cannot change its heat.

स्वभावेनामृतो यस्य भावो गच्छति मर्त्यताम् ।
कृतकेनामृतस्तस्य कथं स्थास्यति निश्चलः ॥२२॥

22. How can an immortal entity continue to be changeless from the standpoint of one according to whom a positive object which is immortal by nature

can pass into birth, it being a product (according to him)?

As for the disputant, *yasya*, according to whom; *bhāvaḥ*, a positive object; which is *svabhāvena amṛtaḥ*, immortal by nature; *gacchati martyatām*, attains transmigratoriness, takes birth in reality; *tasya*, for him, it is a meaningless proposition to hold that entity to be naturally immortal before creation. *Katham*, how, can that entity; be *amṛtaḥ*, immortal; *tasya*, for him; *kṛtakena*, inasmuch as it is a product? Being an effect, how will that immortal *sthāsyati*, continue to be; *niścalaḥ*, unchanging, immortal by nature? It cannot remain so by any means. At no time can there exist anything called an 'unborn' for one who holds the view that the Self has birth; for him all this is mortal. Hence (from this standpoint) we are faced with the negation of freedom. This is the idea.

Objection: For one who holds the view that the Self does not undergo birth, the Vedic passages speaking of creation can have no validity.

Answer: It is true that there are Vedic texts supporting creation, but such passages have some other point in view; and we said that it 'is merely by way of generating the idea' of unity (*Kārikā*, III. 15). Though the objection was disposed of, the contention and its refutation are adverted to here again merely with a view to allaying the doubts as to whether the passages dealing with creation are favourable or opposed to the subject matter that is going to be dealt with:

भूततोऽभूततो वाऽपि सृज्यमाने समा श्रुतिः ।
निश्चितं युक्तियुक्तं च यत्तद्भवति नेतरत् ॥२३॥

23. Vedic texts are equally in evidence with regard to creation in reality and through Māyā. That which is ascertained (by the Vedas) and is supported by reasoning can be the meaning, and nothing else.

Samā śrutiḥ, Vedic texts (speaking of creation) are equally in evidence; *sṛjyamāne*, with regard to a thing being created; *bhūtataḥ*, in reality; *vā*, or; *abhūtataḥ*, through Māyā, as is done by a magician.

Objection: Of the two possible meanings—primary and secondary—it is reasonable to understand a word in its primary sense.

Answer: Not so, for we said earlier that creation in any other sense is not recognized (in our philosophy), and it serves no purpose. All talks of creation, in the primary or secondary sense, relate only to creation through ignorance, and not to creation in reality, as is denied in the Vedic text, 'since He is co-extensive with all that is within and without, and since He has no birth' (Mu. II. i. 2). Therefore that which is *niścitam*, determined, by the Vedas, to be one without a second, birthless, and immortal; *ca*, and; is *yukti-yuktam*, supported by reasoning; *tat*, that, alone; *bhavati*, becomes, the meaning of the Vedic text, and never anything else. This is what we said in the earlier verses.

It is being shown as to what kind of Vedic categorical statements are met with:

नेह नानेति चाम्नायादिन्द्रो मायाभिरित्यपि ।
अजायमानो बहुधा मायया जायते तु सः ॥२४॥

24. Since it is stated (in the Vedas), 'There is no diversity here', and 'The Lord, on account of Māyā, (is perceived as manifold)', '(the Self) without being born (appears to be born in various ways)', it follows that He is born on account of Māyā alone.

If creation had taken place in reality, the diverse things should have been real, and there should not have been any scriptural text showing their unreality. But, as a matter of fact, there are such texts as, 'There is no diversity here whatsoever' (Ka. II. i. 11), which purport to deny the existence of duality. Therefore creation, which has been imagined as a help to the comprehension of non-duality of the Self, is as unreal as the interlogue of Prāṇa (vide *Kārikā*, III. 15); for this creation is referred to by the word Māyā, indicative of unreal things, in the passage, 'The Lord, on account of Māyā (is perceived as manifold)' (Bṛ. II. v. 19).

Objection: The word Māyā implies knowledge.

Answer: True. But even so it is nothing damaging, since sense-knowledge is accepted as a kind of Māyā, it being a product of ignorance. So *māyābhiḥ* (in Bṛ. II. v. 19) means 'through different kinds of sense-knowledge', which are but forms of ignorance, as is proved by the Vedic text, 'Though unborn, It appears to be born in diverse ways' (Y. XXXI. 19). Therefore *saḥ*, He (the Self); *jāyate māyayā tu*, takes birth through Māyā alone, the word *tu* being used to add emphasis thus—'through Māyā to be sure'; for (otherwise) birthlessness and birth in various ways cannot be reconciled in the same thing like heat and cold in fire. Besides, from the fact that realization of unity is a fruitful thing as mentioned in the Vedic text, 'what delusion and what sorrow can there be for that seer of oneness?' (Īś. 7), it follows that the unitive outlook is the definite conclusion of the Upaniṣads, and this view is supported by the fact that in such texts as, 'He goes from death to death who sees as though there is difference here' (Ka. II. i. 11), the idea of heterogeneity, implied by creation etc., is condemned.

संभूतेरपवादाच्च संभवः प्रतिषिध्यते ।
को न्वेनं जनयेदिति कारणं प्रतिषिध्यते ॥२५॥

25. From the refutation of (the worship of) Hiraṇyagarbha, it follows that creation is negated. By the text, 'who should bring him forth?', is ruled out any cause.

Saṁbhavaḥ pratiṣidhyate, creation (i.e. the created things), is negated; *saṁbhūteḥ apavādāt*, because of the denial of the worship of the Majestic One[1] (Hiraṇya-

[1] The Deity that is possessed of full majesty (*sam-bhūti*).

garbha), in the text, 'They enter into blinding darkness who worship the Unmanifested' (Īś. 12). For if Hiraṇyagarbha were absolutely real, there would not have been any denunciation of His (worship).

Objection: The denunciation of (the worship of) Hiraṇyagarbha is meant for bringing about the combination of worship with rites (*vināśa*), as is known from the text, 'They enter into blinding darkness who are engaged in (mere) rites' (Īś. 9).

Answer: It is true that the condemnation of the meditation on (or worship of) Hiraṇyagarbha is meant for enjoining a combination of the meditation on the Deity, viz Hiraṇyagarbha, with rites, referred to by the word *vināśa* (lit. the destructible). Still, just as rites, called *vināśa*, are meant for transcending death consisting in the natural tendencies engendered by ignorance, so also the combination of the meditation on gods with the rites—which is enjoined for the purification of the human heart—is calculated to lead one beyond death that consists in the twofold hankering for ends and means, into which the impulsion, engendered by the craving for the results of works, transforms itself. For thus alone will a man be sanctified by becoming free from the impurity that is the death characterized by the twofold hankering. Therefore this *avidyā* (lit. ignorance), characterized by a combination of the meditation on gods with the rites, aims at leading one beyond death. Thus indeed does the knowledge of the oneness of the supreme Self arise inevitably in one who becomes disgusted with the world, who is ever engaged in the discussion of the

Upaniṣadic truths, and who goes beyond death that is but (a form of) *avidyā* (or ignorance) characterized by the dual desire (for ends and means). Thus, in relation to the pre-existing ignorance, the knowledge of Brahman, leading to immortality, comes as a successor to be related with the same person; and therefore (in this sense) the latter is said to be combined with the former. Accordingly, since the worship of Hiraṇyagarbha is meant to serve a purpose different from that of the knowledge of Brahman leading to immortality, the refutation of the worship of Hiraṇyagarbha is tantamount to its denunciation, and this is so because it has no direct bearing on emancipation, though it is a means of purification. Thus from the condemnation of the worship of Hiraṇyagarbha it follows that He has got only a relative existence; and hence creation, (as symbolized by Hiraṇyagarbha and) called immortality, stands negated from the standpoint of the absolutely real oneness of the Self.

So, since it is the individual soul itself, created by ignorance and existing through ignorance alone, that attains its natural stature on the eradication of ignorance, therefore, in the highest sense, '*Kaḥ nu enam janayet*, who should again bring him forth?' (Bṛ. III. ix. 28.7). For none indeed creates again a snake, superimposed on a rope through ignorance, once it is removed through discrimination. Similarly none will create this individual. By the words, '*kaḥ nu*, who indeed', used with the force of a covert denial; *kāraṇam pratiṣidhyate*, is ruled out any cause. The idea is that a thing that was created by ignorance and (later) disappeared has no source of birth, in accordance with the Vedic text, 'It did not originate from anything, nor did anything originate from It' (Ka. I. ii. 18).

स एष नेति नेतीति व्याख्यातं निह्नुते यतः ।
सर्वमग्राह्यभावेन हेतुनाऽजं प्रकाशते ॥२६॥

26. Since by taking the help of incomprehensibility (of Brahman) as a reason, all that was explained earlier (as a means for the knowledge of Brahman) is negated by the text, 'This Self is that which has been described as "Not this, not this"', therefore the birthless Self becomes self-revealed.

The Upaniṣad thinks that the Self, presented through a negation of all attributes in the text, 'Now, therefore, the description (of Brahman): "Not this, not this"' (Bṛ. II. iii. 6), is very difficult to understand; so, whatever was *vyākhyātam*, explained through various ways for the sake of establishing that very Self again and again; *nihnute*, it negates all that.[1] By

[1] Vide Bṛ. II. iii. 6, III. ix. 26, IV. ii. 4, IV. iv. 22, and IV. v. 15. Bṛ. II. iii, starts with, 'Brahman has but two forms—gross and subtle,' etc. And at the end of the section it is stated, 'Now, therefore, the description (of Brahman): "Not this, not this"'. But though explained once, the Self is very difficult to comprehend. Hence the Upaniṣad adopts other helps to present the same entity and then negates them with 'not this, not this', so that the absolute Brahman alone may be comprehended as the only Reality.

showing in the text, 'This Self is that which has been described as "not this, not this"' (Bṛ. III. ix. 26), that the Self is imperceptible, the Upaniṣad negates, by implication, all that is perceptible, has origination, and is comprehended by the intellect.[1] Being afraid lest people, not cognizant of the fact that anything presented as a means for establishing something else has only that other thing as its goal, should jump to the conclusion that one must cling as firmly to the means as to the end itself, the Upaniṣad *nihnute*, refutes (the idea of the reality of the means); *agrāhyabhāvena hetunā*, by taking the help of the incomprehensibility (of the Self) as a reason. This is the purport. As a result of this, the reality of the Self that is co-extensive with all that is within and without and is *ajam*, birthless; *prakāśate*, gets revealed, by Itself, to one who knows that the means only serves the purpose of the end and that the end has ever the same changeless nature.[2]

Thus the definite conclusion arrived at by hundreds of Vedic texts is that the reality of the Self that is co-extensive with all that exists within and without, and is birthless, is one without a second, and there is

[1] The imperceptible Brahman cannot be the supreme Reality if perceptible things, too, are equally real. Therefore the truth of Brahman implies the unreality of duality.

[2] A superimposed thing has no reality of its own just like a snake imagined on a rope. Similarly, all phenomenal things like specific attributes that are denied in Brahman, have no existence by the very fact of being negated. It is a mistake to think that the negated counterpart of this negation must also be true.

nothing besides. It is now said that this very fact is established by reason as well:

सतो हि मायया जन्म युज्यते न तु तत्त्वतः।
तत्त्वतो जायते यस्य जातं तस्य हि जायते ॥२७॥

27. Birth of a thing that (already) exists can reasonably be possible only through Māyā and not in reality. For one who holds that things take birth in a real sense, there can only be the birth of what is already born.

With regard to the Reality that is the Self, the apprehension may arise that, if it be incomprehensible for ever, It may as well be non-existent. But that is not correct, for Its effect is perceptible. As the effect consisting in *janma*, birth (of things); *māyayā*, through magic; follows *sataḥ*, from (the magician) who exists; so the perceptible effect in the form of the birth of the world leads one to assume a Self existing in the highest sense, which like the magician is the basis for the Māyā consisting in the origination of the world; for it is but reasonable to think that like such effects as elephants etc., produced with the help of magic, the creation of the universe proceeds *sataḥ*, from some cause that has existence, and not from an unreal one. But it is not reasonable to say that from the birthless Self there can be any birth *tattvataḥ*, in reality. Or the meaning is this: As the *janma*, birth, in the form of a snake etc.; *sataḥ*, of an existing thing, a rope for instance; *yujyate*, can reasonably be; *māyayā*, through Māyā, but not *tattvataḥ*, in reality; similarly, though the Self that exists is incomprehensible, It can reasonably have birth in the form of the universe through Māyā like the illusion of a snake on a rope; but the birthless Self cannot have any birth in the real sense. *Yasya*, as for the disputant, again, who holds that the unborn Self, the supreme Reality; *jāyate*, undergoes birth, as the universe, he cannot make such an absurd assertion that the birthless passes into birth since this involves a contradiction. Hence he has to admit perforce that *jātam*, what is already born; *jāyate*, takes birth, again; and from this predication of birth from what is born will follow an infinite regress. Therefore it is established that the Reality that is the Self, is birthless and one.

असतो मायया जन्म तत्त्वतो नैव युज्यते।
बन्ध्यापुत्रो न तत्त्वेन मायया वाऽपि जायते॥२८॥

28. There can be no birth for a non-existent object either through Māyā or in reality, for the son of a barren woman is born neither through Māyā nor in reality.

For those who think everything to be unreal, *janma na yujyate*, there can be no possibility of birth, in any way; *asataḥ*, of a non-existent object; *māyayā tattvataḥ vā*, either through Māyā or in reality, for such is never our experience. For *bandhyāputraḥ*, the son of a barren woman; *na jāyate*, never takes birth; either through Māyā or in reality. Hence the theory of nihilism is entirely out of place in the present context. This is the idea.

How, again, can there be birth for the existent through Māyā alone? That is being explained:

यथा स्वप्ने द्वयाभासं स्पन्दते मायया मनः।
तथा जाग्रद्द्वयाभासं स्पन्दते मायया मनः ॥२९॥

29. As in dream the mind vibrates, as though having dual aspects, so in the waking state the mind vibrates as though with two facets.

As the snake imagined on a rope is true when seen as the rope, so *manaḥ*, the mind, is true when seen as the Self, the supreme Consciousness. As like a snake appearing on a rope, the mind *spandate*, vibrates; *svapne*, in dream; *māyayā*, through Māyā; *dvayābhāsam*, as if possessed of two facets—the cognizer and the thing cognized; *tathā*, just like that; *jāgrat*, in the waking state; *manaḥ*, the mind; *spandate*, vibrates, as it were; *māyayā*, through Māyā.

अद्वयं च द्वयाभासं मनः स्वप्ने न संशयः।
अद्वयं च द्वयाभासं तथा जाग्रन्न संशयः ॥३०॥

30. There is no doubt that in dream, the mind, though one, appears in dual aspects; so also in the waking state, the mind, though one, appears to have two aspects.

Na saṁśayaḥ, there is no doubt; that just as the snake is true in its aspect of the rope, so the *manas*, mind; that is but *advayam*, non-dual, in its aspect of the Self from the highest standpoint; *dvayābhāsam*, appears to have two aspects; *svapne*, in dream. For apart from Consciousness, there do not exist two things in dream —elephants and so on that are perceived and eyes and the rest that perceive them. The idea is that the case is similar in the waking state also; for in either state there exists only the supremely real Consciousness.[1]

It has been said that it is the mind alone which, like a snake on a rope, appears as an illusion, in dual roles. What proof is there as to that? The text advances (inferential) proof on the basis of agreement and difference. How?

मनोदृश्यमिदं द्वैतं यत्किंचित्सचराचरम् ।
मनसो ह्यमनीभावे द्वैतं नैवोपलभ्यते ॥३१॥

31. All this that there is—together with all that moves or does not move—is perceived by the mind (and therefore all this is but the mind); for when the mind ceases to be the mind, duality is no longer perceived.

'*Idam dvaitam*, this duality, as a whole; that is *mano-dṛśyam*, perceived by the mind; is nothing but the mind, which is itself imagined (on the Self)'—this is the proposition. For duality endures so long as the mind does, and disappears with the disappearance of

[1] The mind fancied on Consciousness through ignorance, vibrates on the supremely real and constant Consciousness in either state.

the mind. *Hi*, for; *manasaḥ amanībhāve*, when the mind ceases to be the mind, when, like the illusory snake disappearing in the rope, the mind's activity stops through the practice of discriminating insight and detachment, or when the mind gets absorbed in the state of sleep; *dvaitam na upalabhyate*, duality is not perceived. From this non-existence is proved the unreality of duality. This is the purport.

How does the mind cease to be the mind? This is being answered:

आत्मसत्यानुबोधेन न सङ्कल्पयते यदा।
अमनस्तां तदा याति ग्राह्याभावे तदग्रहम् ॥३२॥

32. When following the instruction of scriptures and the teacher, the mind ceases to think as a consequence of the realization of the Truth that is the Self, then the mind attains the state of not being the mind; in the absence of things to be perceived, it becomes a non-perceiver.

Ātmasatya: the Truth that is Self, which is comparable to the reality of earth as stated in the Vedic text, 'All transformation has speech as its basis, and it is name only. Earth as such is the reality' (Ch. VI. i. 4). *Ātmasatya-anubodha* is the realization of that Truth of the Self which follows from the instruction of scriptures and the teacher. *Yadā*, when, as a consequence of that, there remains nothing to be thought of; and the mind *na saṅkalpayate*, does not think—as fire does not burn in the absence of combustible things;

tadā, then, at that time; *yāti amanastām*, it attains the state of ceasing to be the mind. *Grāhyābhāve*, in the absence of things to be perceived; *tat*, that mind; *agraham*, becomes free from all illusion of perceptions. This is the idea.

If this duality be false, how is the truth of one's own Self realized? The answer is:

अकल्पकमजं ज्ञानं ज्ञेयाभिन्नं प्रचक्षते ।
ब्रह्मज्ञेयमजं नित्यमजेनाजं विबुध्यते ॥३३॥

33. They say that the non-conceptual knowledge, which is birthless, is non-different from the knowable (Brahman). The knowledge that has Brahman for its content is birthless and everlasting. The birthless (Self) is known by the birthless (knowledge).

The knowers of Brahman *pracakṣate*, say; that absolute *jñānam*, knowledge; which is *akalpakam*, devoid of all imagination (non-conceptual); and is therefore *ajam*, birthless; is *jñeyābhinnam*, non-different from the knowable, identified with Brahman, the absolute Reality. And this is supported by such Vedic texts as, 'for the knower's function of knowing can never be lost' (Bṛ. IV. iii. 30), like the heat of fire; 'Knowledge, Bliss, Brahman' (Bṛ. III. ix. 28. 7); 'Brahman is truth, knowledge, infinite' (Tai. II. i. 1). The phrase *brahma-jñeyam*, is an attribute of that very knowledge, and means that very knowledge of which Brahman Itself is the content and which is non-different from Brahman, as heat is from fire. By that *ajena*, unborn, knowledge, which is the very nature of the Self; *vibudhyate*, is known—It knows by Itself; the *ajam*, birthless Reality, which is the Self. The idea conveyed is that the Self being ever a homogeneous mass of Consciousness, like the sun that is by nature a constant light, does not depend on any other knowledge (for Its revelation).

It has been said that when the mind is divested of ideation by virtue of the realization of the Truth that is Brahman, and when there is an absence of external objects (of perception), it becomes tranquil, controlled, and withdrawn like fire that has no fuel. And it has further been said that when the mind thus ceases to be the mind, duality also disappears.

निगृहीतस्य मनसो निर्विकल्पस्य धीमतः ।
प्रचारः स तु विज्ञेयः सुषुप्तेऽन्यो न तत्समः ॥३४॥

34. The behaviour that the mind has when it is under control, free from all ideation, and full of discrimination, should be particularly noted. The behaviour of the mind in deep sleep is different and is not similar to that (of the controlled mind).

Pracārah, the behaviour, that there is; *manasaḥ*, of the mind; *nigṛhītasya*, which is (thus) under control; *nirvikalpasya*, which is free from all ideation; *dhīmataḥ*, which is full of discrimination; *saḥ* that behaviour; *vijñeyaḥ*, is to be particularly noted, by the Yogis.

Objection: In the absence of all kinds of awareness, the mind under control behaves in the same way as the mind in sleep. Hence the absence of awareness being the same, what is there to be particularly noted?

With regard to this the *answer* is: The objection is untenable, since the behaviour of the mind *suṣupte*, in deep sleep; is *anyaḥ*, different; the mind being then under the cover of the darkness of delusion arising from ignorance, and it being still possessed of the latent tendencies that are the seeds of many evil actions. And the behaviour of the mind under control is surely different, since ignorance, the seed of evil activities, has been burnt away from that mind by the fire of the realization of the Truth that is the Self, and since from that mind has been removed the blemish of all afflictions. Hence (the sleeping mind's behaviour) *na tatsamaḥ*, is not like that behaviour (in the controlled state). Therefore it is fit to be known. This is the meaning.

The reason for the difference of behaviour is being stated:

लीयते हि सुषुप्ते तन्निगृहीतं न लीयते ।
तदेव निर्भयं ब्रह्म ज्ञानालोकं समन्ततः ॥३५॥

35. For that mind loses itself in sleep, but does not lose itself when under control. That very mind becomes the fearless Brahman, possessed of the light of Consciousness all around.

Hi, since; *suṣupte*,[1] in deep sleep; *tat*, that, the mind

[1] A different reading is *suṣuptau*.

together with all its tendencies and impressions that are the seeds of all such mental modes as ignorance (egoism, attachment) etc.; *līyate*, loses itself, attains a seed-state of potentiality which is a kind of darkness and non-differentiation; but when that mind is *nigrhītam*, withdrawn, through knowledge arising from discrimination; *na līyate*, it does not lose itself, it does not attain the seed-state of darkness; therefore it is reasonable that the behaviours of the sleeping and controlled minds should be different. *Tat eva*, that very mind; becomes the supreme non-dual *brahma*, Brahman Itself; when (in its absorption in Brahman) it is freed from the dual taint of being the subject and the object which are the creations of ignorance. Since this is the case, therefore that very mind becomes *nirbhayam*, fearless; for then there is no perception of duality that causes fear (cf. Bṛ. I. iv. 2). Brahman is that quiescent and fearless entity, by knowing which one has no fear from anywhere (cf. Tai. II. ix). That Brahman is being further distinguished: *Jñāna* means Knowledge, Consciousness, which is the very nature of the Self; and Brahman which has that Knowledge as Its *ālokaḥ*, light (expression) is *jñānālokam*, possessed of the light of Knowledge. The meaning is that It is a homogeneous mass of Consciousness, *samantataḥ*, all around; i.e. like space, It is all-pervasive without a break.

अजमनिद्रमस्वप्नमनामकमरूपकम् ।
सकृद्विभातं सर्वज्ञं नोपचारः कथञ्चन ॥३६॥

36. Brahman is birthless, sleepless, dreamless,

nameless, formless, ever effulgent, everything, and a knower. (With regard to It) there is not the least possibility of ceremony.

Brahman which coexists with all that is inside and outside, is *ajam*, unborn, since It has no source of birth. We said that birth is verily caused by ignorance as in the case of a snake on a rope; and that ignorance is nullified on the realization of the truth of the Self according to instruction. As It is birthless, so It is *anidram*, sleepless. Sleep is the beginningless Māyā characterized by ignorance. Since he (man) has awakened into his own real, non-dual nature that is the Self, therefore he is *asvapnam*, dreamless. And since his name and form are creations of the state of non-waking, and they are destroyed on waking up like the illusion of a snake on a rope, therefore Brahman cannot be named by any word, nor can It be described as having any form in any way; thus It is also *anāmakam arūpakam*, without name and form, as is stated by the Vedic text, 'From which words turn back' (Tai. II. iv, II. ix). Moreover, It is *sakṛt vibhātam*, ever illumined, constant effulgence by nature, since It is devoid of non-manifestation that is consequent on non-perception, and devoid of manifestation that is contingent on wrong perception (as in the case of an individual[1]). Realization and non-realization (of

[1] In an individual, Brahman is said to be hidden when it is not perceived as 'I'. And when a false perception arises in the form 'I am an agent' etc., Brahman is said to be manifest. When these two ideas are absent, Brahman remains as the Self-effulgent Reality.

Brahman) are as day and night (of the sun[1]), and the darkness of nescience is ever the cause of non-manifestation. Since this is absent from Brahman, and since Brahman is by nature the light that is eternal Consciousness, it is but reasonable that It should be constantly effulgent. Hence, too, It is *sarva-jñam*: *sarva*, all, as well as, *jña*, a knower, by nature. With regard to this Brahman of such characteristics there can be *na upacāraḥ*, no ceremony (practice) as others have, e.g. concentration of mind etc. that are different from the nature of the Self. The idea is this: As Brahman is by nature eternally pure, intelligent, and free, there can be no possibility of anything to be done (by the enlightened person) *kathañcana*, in any way whatsoever, after the destruction of ignorance.

The reason is being adduced for establishing namelessness etc. mentioned above:

सर्वाभिलापविगतः सर्वचिन्तासमुत्थितः ।
सुप्रशान्तः सकृज्ज्योतिः समाधिरचलोऽभयः ॥३७॥

37. The Self is free of all sense-organs, and is above all internal organs. It is supremely tranquil, eternal effulgence, divine absorption, immutable, and fearless.

The word *abhilāpaḥ*, derived in the sense of that by

[1] True it is that non-realization precedes and realization succeeds instruction. But they do not belong to Brahman. The sun is supposed to be subject to day and night, because people fancy the sun to rise and set. But in reality the sun has no night or day. Similarly, Brahman has no realization or non-realization.

which utterance is made, refers to the organ of speech, the means of expressing all kinds of words. It is (*vigataḥ*) free from that (organ of speech). Speech is here used suggestively. So the meaning implied is that It is free of all external organs. Similarly, It is *sarva-cintā-samutthitaḥ*: The word *cintā*, derived in the sense of that by which things are thought of, means the intellect; *samutthitaḥ* means risen above that; that is to say, It is devoid of the internal organ, which accords with the Vedic text, '. . . therefore He is without vital force and without mind; He is pure and superior to the (other) superior imperishable' (Mu. II. i. 2). Being devoid of all objects, It is *supraśāntaḥ*, absolutely tranquil; *sakṛjjyotiḥ*, everlasting light, by virtue of being by nature the Consciousness that is the Self; *samādhiḥ*, divine absorption—so called since It is realizable through the insight arising out of the deepest concentration (*samādhi*). Or It is called *samādhi*, because It is the object of concentration. It is *acalaḥ*, immutable; and therefore *abhayaḥ*, fearless, since there is no mutation.

Since Brahman Itself has been described as divine absorption, immutable, and fearless, therefore—

ग्रहो न तत्र नोत्सर्गश्चिन्ता यत्र न विद्यते।
आत्मसंस्थं तदा ज्ञानमजाति समतां गतम् ॥३८॥

38. There can be no acceptance or rejection where all mentation stops. Then knowledge is established in the Self and is unborn, and it becomes homogeneous.

Tatra, there, in that Brahman; *vidyate*, there exists;

na grahaḥ, no acceptance; *na utsargaḥ*, no rejection or loss; for acceptance or rejection is possible where mutability or the possibility of it exists. These two are incompatible here with Brahman, for nothing else exists in It to cause a change, and It is without parts. Therefore there is no rejection or acceptance in It; *yatra*, where; *cintā*, thought (mentation); *na vidyate*, does not exist. This is the idea. That is to say, how can there be rejection or acceptance where no mentation is possible in the absence of the mind? As soon as there comes the realization of the Truth that is the Self, *tadā*, then, in the absence of any object (to be known); *jñānam*, knowledge; is *ātmasaṁstham*, established in the Self, like the heat of fire in fire (when there is no fuel). It is then *ajāti*, birthless; and *gatam samatām*, becomes homogeneous.

The promise which was made earlier, 'Hence I shall speak of Brahman which is free from limitation, is without birth, and is in the state of homogeneity' (*Kārikā*, III. 2), and which has been fulfilled with the help of scripture and reasoning, is concluded here by saying, 'unborn, and it becomes homogeneous'. Everything else, apart from this realization of the Self, is within the sphere of misery, as is declared by the Vedic text, 'O Gārgī, he, who departs from this world without knowing this Immutable, is miserable' (Bṛ. III. viii. 10). The meaning sought to be conveyed is that by knowing this, one becomes a Brāhmaṇa (knower of Brahman) and has one's duties fulfilled.

Though this supreme Reality is such, yet—

अस्पर्शयोगो वै नाम दुर्दर्शः सर्वयोगिभिः ।
योगिनो बिभ्यति ह्यस्मादभये भयदर्शिनः ॥३९॥

39. The Yoga that is familiarly referred to as 'contactless' is difficult to be comprehended by any-one of the Yogis. For those Yogis, who apprehend fear where there is no fear, are afraid of it.

Asparśa-yogaḥ nāma, this is familiar as the Yoga which is contactless, since it has no relation, indicated by the word *contact*, with anything; *vai*, (this is how it is) referred to, well known in all the Upaniṣads. It is *durdarśaḥ*, hard to be seen; *sarvayogibhiḥ*, by all the Yogis, who are devoid of the knowledge imparted in the Upaniṣads. The idea is that it is attainable only through the effort involved in the realization of the Self in accordance with instruction. *Hi*, for; *yoginaḥ*, the Yogis; who are *bhayadarśinaḥ abhaye*, perceivers of fear in this fearless (Brahman), the non-discriminating ones who apprehend the destruction of their personality, which fact becomes the cause of their fear; (they) *asmāt bibhyati*, are afraid of it, thinking this Yoga to be the same as the disintegration of their own individuality, though in fact it is beyond all fear.

But for those to whom the mind and the sense-organs etc., which are imagined like a snake on a rope, have no existence in reality when considered apart from their essence that is Brahman—for those who have become identified with Brahman—comes fearlessness; and for them naturally is accomplished the everlasting peace called emancipation which is not dependent on any other factor, as we declared earlier in, 'there is not the least possibility of ceremony' (*Kārikā*, III. 36). But, for the Yogis who are other than these, who are still treading the path, who have inferior or medium outlook and think of the mind as something different from the Self, though associated with It — for those who are not possessed of the realization of the Self that is the Truth —

मनसो निग्रहायत्तमभयं सर्वयोगिनाम् ।
दुःखक्षयः प्रबोधश्चाप्यक्षया शान्तिरेव च ॥४०॥

40. For all these Yogis, fearlessness, the removal of misery, knowledge (of the Self), and everlasting peace are dependent on the control of the mind.

Sarvayoginām, for all Yogis; *abhayam*, fearlessness; is *manasaḥ nigrahāyattam*, contingent on the control of the mind; and so also is *duḥkhakṣayaḥ*, the removal of misery. For there can be no extinction of sorrow for the non-discriminating people so long as the mind, which has association with the Self, continues to be disturbed. Moreover, (for them) the knowledge of the Self, too, is contingent on the control of the mind. Similarly, *akṣayā śāntiḥ*, the everlasting peace, called Liberation, is also certainly dependent on the control of the mind.

उत्सेक उदधेर्यद्वत्कुशाग्रेणैकबिन्दुना ।
मनसो निग्रहस्तद्वद्भवेदपरिखेदतः ॥४१॥

41. Just as an ocean can be emptied with the help

of the tip of a blade of Kuśa grass that can hold just a drop, so also can the control of the mind be brought about by absence of depression.

Even the control of the mind comes about *aparikhedataḥ*, from the want of depression; for those Yogis whose minds are free from mental depression, and who are as relentless as in trying to empty an ocean; *kuśāgreṇa ekabindunā*, with the help of the tip of a blade of Kuśa grass that can hold only a drop. This is the idea.

Is diligence alone, that knows no depression, the means for controlling the mind? The answer is being given negatively:

उपायेन निगृह्णीयाद्विक्षिप्तं कामभोगयोः ।
सुप्रसन्नं लये चैव यथा कामो लयस्तथा ॥४२॥

42. With the help of that proper process one should bring under discipline the mind that remains dispersed amidst objects of desire and enjoyment; and one should bring it under control even when it is in full peace in sleep, for sleep is as bad as desire.

Being armed with untiring effort, and taking for aid the means to be stated, *nigṛhṇīyāt*, one should bring under discipline, i.e. concentrate on the Self Itself; the mind that remains *vikṣiptam*, dispersed, amidst objects of desire and their enjoyment. Moreover, *laya* means that in which anything gets merged, i.e. sleep. Though the mind be *suprasannam*, very peaceful, i.e. free from effort; *laye*, in that sleep; still 'it should be brought under discipline'—this much has to be supplied. Should it be asked, 'If it is fully at peace, why should it be disciplined?' the answer is: 'Since *layaḥ tathā*, sleep is as much a source of evil; *yathā kāmaḥ*, as desire is.' So the idea implied is this: As the mind engaged in objects of desire is to be controlled, so also is the mind in sleep to be disciplined.

Which is that process? That is being stated:

दुःखं सर्वमनुस्मृत्य कामभोगान्निवर्तयेत् ।
अजं सर्वमनुस्मृत्य जातं नैव तु पश्यति ॥४३॥

43. Constantly remembering that everything is full of misery, one should withdraw the mind from the enjoyment arising out of desire. Remembering ever the fact that the birthless Brahman is everything, one does not surely perceive the born (viz the host of duality).

Anusmṛtya, remembering, the fact that; *sarvam*, everything, all duality that is created by ignorance; is *duḥkham*, full of sorrow; *nivartayet*, one should withdraw, the mind; *kāmabhogāt*, from enjoyment prompted by desire, from the objects of desire; one should withdraw with the help of ideas of detachment—this is the meaning. *Anusmṛtya*, remembering the fact, from the instruction of scriptures and the teacher; that *ajam*, the birthless, Brahman; is *sarvam*, everything; *na eva tu paśyati*, one does not certainly perceive, the host of duality that is opposed to Brahman; for duality ceases then.

लये संबोधयेच्चित्तं विक्षिप्तं शमयेत्पुनः ।
सकषायं विजानीयात्समप्राप्तं न चालयेत् ॥४४॥

44. One should wake up the mind merged in deep sleep; one should bring the dispersed mind into tranquillity again; one should know when the mind is tinged with desire (and is in a state of latency). One should not disturb the mind established in equipoise.

Thus with the help of the dual process of detachment and practice of knowledge, *saṁbodhayet*, one should wake up; the mind merged *laye*, in deep sleep; one should engage it in the realization of the transcendence of the Self. The word *citta* has the same meaning as *manas*, mind. *Śamayet punaḥ*, one should again make tranquil; the mind that is *vikṣiptam*, dispersed, amidst desire and enjoyment. When the mind of a man, who is practising again and again, is awakened from deep sleep and is withdrawn from objects, but is not established in equipoise and continues in an intermediate state, then *vijānīyāt*, one should know; that mind to be *sakaṣāyam*, tinged with desire, in a state of latency. From that state, too, it should be diligently led to equipoise. But when the mind becomes *samaprāptam*, equipoised, that is to say, when it begins to move toward that goal; *na vicālayet*, one should not disturb it from that course; or in other words, one should not turn it back toward objects.

नास्वादयेत्सुखं तत्र निःसङ्गः प्रज्ञया भवेत् ।
निश्चलं निश्चरच्चित्तमेकीकुर्यात्प्रयत्नतः ॥४५॥

45. One should not enjoy happiness in that state; but one should become unattached through the use of discrimination. When the mind, established in steadiness, wants to issue out, one should concentrate it with diligence.

The *sukham*, happiness, which a Yogi gets while trying to concentrate his mind; *na āsvādayet*, he should not enjoy; that is to say, he should not get attached *tatra*, there, to that state. How should he behave there? He should become *niḥsaṅgaḥ*, unattached; *prajñayā*, through the discriminating intellect. He should think, 'Whatever happiness is perceived is a creation of ignorance, and it is false.' He should also withdraw his mind from that kind of attraction for joy—this is the purport. When having been withdrawn from the attraction for happiness, and having attained the state of steadiness, the mind becomes *niścarat*, intent on going out; then withdrawing it from those objects with the help of the above-mentioned process, one *ekīkuryāt*, should diligently concentrate it—in the Self itself; *prayatnataḥ*, with diligence. The idea is that it should be made to attain its true nature of Consciousness alone.

यदा न लीयते चित्तं न च विक्षिप्यते पुनः ।
अनिङ्गनमनाभासं निष्पन्नं ब्रह्म तत्तदा ॥४६॥

46. When the mind does not become lost nor is scattered, when it is motionless and does not appear in the form of objects, then it becomes Brahman.

Yadā, when; the *cittam*, mind; brought under control through the aforesaid process, *na līyate*, does not become lost, in sleep; and also *na ca punaḥ vikṣipyate*, does not, again, become dispersed, amidst objects; and when the mind becomes *aniṅganam*, motionless, like a lamp in a windless place; and *anābhāsam*, does not appear in the form of any fancied object; when the mind assumes such characteristics, then it *niṣpannam brahma*, becomes Brahman; or in other words, the mind then becomes identified with Brahman.

स्वस्थं शान्तं सनिर्वाणमकथ्यं सुखमुत्तमम् ।
अजमजेन ज्ञेयेन सर्वज्ञं परिचक्षते ॥४७॥

47. That highest Bliss is located in one's own Self. It is quiescent, coexistent with liberation, beyond description, and birthless. And since It is identical with the unborn knowable (Brahman), they call It the Omniscient (Brahman).

The above-mentioned Bliss, which is the highest Reality, and which consists in the realization of the Truth that is the Self, is *svastham*, located in one's own Self; *śāntam*, quiescent, characterized by the absence of all evil; *sanirvāṇam*, coexistent with cessation, i.e. liberation; and it is *akathyam*, indescribable, as it relates to an absolutely unique entity; it is *uttamam sukham*, the highest happiness, it being unsurpassable and open to the vision of the Yogis alone. It is *ajam*, unborn, unlike objective happiness. And since this happiness, in its true nature of omniscience, is identical *ajena*, with the unborn; *jñeyena*, (with the) thing to be known; therefore the knowers of Brahman *paricakṣate*, call it; *sarvajñam*, the omniscient one, Brahman Itself.

All such ideas—e.g. the control of the mind and so on, creation resembling the evolution of forms from earth and gold, and meditation—have been spoken of as the means leading to the realization of the supreme Reality as It is in Itself; but these have not been spoken of as supremely true in themselves. The absolutely highest Truth, however, is:

न कश्चिज्जायते जीवः संभवोऽस्य न विद्यते।
एतत्तदुत्तमं सत्यं यत्र किञ्चिन्न जायते ॥४८॥

48. No individual being, whichsoever, takes birth. It has no source (of birth). This (Brahman) is that highest Truth where nothing whatsoever takes birth.

Na jīvaḥ kaḥ cit, no individual being whichsoever, who is a doer or an enjoyer; *jāyate*, is born, by any means whatsoever. Hence for the Self that is naturally unborn and non-dual, *na vidyate*, there does not exist; any *saṁbhavaḥ*, source, cause (for undergoing birth). Since there does not exist for It any cause, therefore no individual being, whichsoever, undergoes birth. This is the meaning. As compared with the truths mentioned earlier as the means, *etat*, this one; is *uttamam satyam*, the highest Truth; (*yatra*) where, in which Brahman that is Truth by nature, *na kiñcit jāyate*, nothing whatsoever, not even a jot or tittle, is born.

CHAPTER IV

ALĀTAŚĀNTI-PRAKARAṆA
(ON QUENCHING THE FIREBRAND)

In the course of determining the meaning of *Om*, non-duality was advanced as a premiss on the basis of the scriptures; it was proved to be true on the basis of the fact that the differences found in things external are unreal; it was again directly determined with the help of scriptures and reason in the chapter on non-duality; and that non-duality was summed up in the concluding remark, 'This is that highest Truth' (*Kārikā*, III. 48). The dualists and the nihilists are opposed to that unitive outlook that is the import of the scriptures. And it has been hinted that their philosophy is false, since their outlook is affected by such vitiating factors as attachment and aversion arising from mutual opposition. And the philosophy of non-duality is extolled inasmuch as it is not subject to such mental perversion. Now begins the chapter on quenching the firebrand, in order to show in detail how those are partial philosophies owing to their mutual contradiction, and then, after rejecting them, to sum up by proving the truth of the philosophy of non-duality with the help of the method of difference (consisting in their rejection[1]). Now while on

[1] Instances of the application of the methods of agreement and difference are: 'Whatever is a product is impermanent', and

this subject, this first verse is meant as a salutation to the promulgator of the school of non-duality by identifying him with non-duality itself. For it is desirable to worship one's teacher at the commencement of a scripture so that the result aimed at may be achieved.

ज्ञानेनाकाशकल्पेन धर्मान्यो गगनोपमान् ।
ज्ञेयाभिन्नेन संबुद्धस्तं वन्दे द्विपदां वरम् ॥१॥

1. I bow down to the One who is the chief among all persons, who has known fully the souls resembling (infinite) sky, through his knowledge that is comparable to space and is non-different from the object of knowledge.

Ākāśakalpa is that which is slightly different from space, that is to say, resembling space. So, *jñānena ākāśakalpena* means 'by a knowledge that is comparable to (infinite) space'. What purpose is served by it? (He knows) *dharmān*, the souls. Souls of what kind? The souls that are *gagana-upamān*, comparable to the sky. There is another qualification of that very knowledge: The knowledge that is *jñeyābhinna*, non-different from the objects of knowledge, viz the souls —just as heat is from fire, or light is from the sun.

'Whatever is not impermanent is not a product'. When both the methods can be applied to a case, all doubts about the truth of the general proposition is set at rest. In the present case, non-duality, presented by the scripture and proved to be a possibility by logic, is confirmed by showing the hollowness of others' views.

He who *saṁbuddhaḥ*, has completely realized; *dharmān gaganopamān*, the entities that are comparable to the sky; *jñeyābhinnena jñānena*, through the knowledge that is non-different from the object of knowledge — which is comparable to space and is non-different from the true nature of the Self that is to be known; He indeed is the Lord called Nārāyaṇa. *Tam vande*, Him I salute; *dvipadām varam*, the greatest among the bipeds, that is to say, the supreme Person among all persons who are suggested by the word 'biped'. Under the garb of this salutation to the teacher, it is suggested that the purpose of this chapter is to establish, through a refutation of the opposite views, the philosophy of the supreme Reality that is devoid of the distinctions of knowledge, knowable, and knower.

Now for extolling the Yoga taught in the philosophy of non-dualism comes a salutation to it:

अस्पर्शयोगो वै नाम सर्वसत्त्वसुखो हितः।
अविवादोऽविरुद्धश्च देशितस्तं नमाम्यहम् ॥२॥

2. I bow down to that Yoga that is well known as free from relationships, joyful to all beings, beneficial, free from dispute, non-contradictory, and set forth in the scriptures.

Asparśa-yogaḥ is that Yoga which has no *sparśa*, touch, relationship, with anything at any time; it is of the very nature of Brahman. To the knowers of Brahman it is *vai nāma*, indeed so named; that is to say, it is well known as the Yoga free from all relationships. And it becomes *sarva-sattva-sukhaḥ*, a bliss to all beings. Some Yoga, as for instance austerity, may itself be sorrowful, though it is distinguished as a means leading to extreme happiness. But this one is not of that sort. What then? It is joyful to all beings. Similarly, in this world, a particular kind of enjoyment of objects may be joyful but not beneficial. But this one is joyful as well as *hitaḥ*, beneficial, since its nature is ever unchanging. Moreover, it is *avivādaḥ*: that in which there is no dispute (*vivāda*) by embracing two sides, for and against, is *avivādaḥ*, free from dispute. Why? Because it is, in addition, *aviruddhaḥ*, non-contradictory. The Yoga of this kind that has been *deśitaḥ*, instructed, by the scripture; *tam*, to that; *aham namāmi*, I make my salutation, i.e. I bow down.

How the dualists contradict each other is being stated:

भूतस्य जातिमिच्छन्ति वादिनः केचिदेव हि।
अभूतस्यापरे धीरा विवदन्तः परस्परम् ॥३॥

3. Only some disputants postulate the birth of a (pre-) existing thing. Other wise ones, while disputing among themselves, postulate the birth of what does not pre-exist.

Hi kecit eva vādinaḥ, only some disputants, viz the Sāṁkhyas; *icchanti*, postulate; *jātim*, the birth; *bhūtasya*, of an existing thing; but not so do all the dualists, for there are *apare*, others, viz the Vaiśeṣikas and the Naiyāyikas; who are *dhīrāḥ*, wise, that is to say, proud of their wisdom; and who while *vivadantaḥ*, talking contrariwise; postulate the birth *abhūtasya*, of a non-existing thing. The idea is that they want to conquer each other through disputation.

Now is being shown what is virtually asserted by them as they refute each other's point of view by talking contrariwise:

भूतं न जायते किंचिदभूतं नैव जायते ।
विवदन्तोऽद्वया ह्येवमजातिं ख्यापयन्ति ते ॥४॥

4. A thing that already exists does not pass into birth; and a thing that does not pre-exist cannot pass into birth. These people, while disputing thus, are really non-dualists, and they thus reveal the absence of birth.

'*Kim cit*, anything; that is *bhūtam*, pre-existing; *na jāyate*, does not pass into birth, just because it exists, as it is in the case of the Self'—while speaking thus, the holder[1] of the view that the effect does not exist before its birth, refutes the view of the Sāṁkhya who says that the effect, pre-existing in the cause,[2] takes birth. Similarly, the Sāṁkhya, too, while speaking thus, '*Abhūtam*, a non-existing—like the horns of a hare; *na eva jāyate*, can never be born, because of the

[1] The Naiyāyika, who virtually subscribes to the view that something comes out of nothing.

[2] The effect remaining involved in the cause.

very fact that it does not exist'—refutes the birth of a non-existing thing as held by those who believe in the non-existence of the effect before production. While *vivadantaḥ*, talking contrariwise; these *advayāḥ*,[1] non-dualists—for these really walk into the camp of the non-dualists by refuting each other's view about the birth of the pre-existing or the non-pre-existing; *khyāpayanti*, reveal, by implication; *ajātim*, the absence of birth itself.

ख्याप्यमानामजातिं तैरनुमोदामहे वयम् ।
विवदामो न तैः सार्धमविवादं निबोधत ॥५॥

5. We approve the birthlessness that is revealed by them; we do not quarrel with them. (O disciples), understand this (philosophy) that is free from dispute.

By saying, 'Let this be so', we simply *anumodāmahe*, approve; the *ajātim*, birthlessness; *taiḥ khyāpyamānām*, thus revealed by them; we *na vivadāmaḥ*, do not quarrel; *taiḥ sārdham*, with them, by taking any side for or against, as they do in regard to each other. This is the idea. Therefore, O disciples, *nibodhata*, understand; that philosophy of the highest Reality that is *avivādam*, beyond dispute, and is approved by us.

अजातस्यैव धर्मस्य जातिमिच्छन्ति वादिनः ।
अजातो ह्यमृतो धर्मो मर्त्यतां कथमेष्यति ॥६॥

[1]Another reading is '*dvayāḥ*, dualists'.

6. The talkers verily vouch for the birth of an unborn positive entity. But how can a positive entity that is unborn and immortal undergo mortality?

Vādinaḥ, the disputants—all of them, whether holding the view of the prior existence or non-existence of the effect. This verse was commented on earlier (*Kārikā*, III. 20).

न भवत्यमृतं मर्त्यं न मर्त्यममृतं तथा ।
प्रकृतेरन्यथाभावो न कथंचिद्भविष्यति ॥७॥

7. The immortal can not become mortal. Similarly the mortal cannot become immortal. The mutation of one's nature will take place in no way whatsoever.

स्वभावेनामृतो यस्य धर्मो गच्छति मर्त्यताम् ।
कृतकेनामृतस्तस्य कथं स्थास्यति निश्चलः ॥८॥

8. How can an immortal entity continue to be changeless from the standpoint of one according to whom a positive entity which is immortal by nature can pass into birth, it being a product (according to him)?

The verses already explained earlier (*Kārikā*, III. 21-22) are quoted here in order to show the confirmation of birthlessness that is revealed through the mutual dispute of other schools of thought.

Inasmuch as one's nature, even in the ordinary

sense of the term, does not change, (far less can the supreme nature change itself). It is being shown what the nature is:

सांसिद्धिकी स्वाभाविकी सहजा अकृता च या।
प्रकृतिः सेति विज्ञेया स्वभावं न जहाति या ॥९॥

9. By the word 'nature' is to be understood that which is permanently acquired, or is intrinsic, instinctive, non-produced, or unchanging in its character.

Saṁsiddhiḥ means complete attainment, and anything resulting from that is *sāṁsiddikī*, as is the nature of the successful Yogis who are endowed with such occult powers of becoming at will subtle like atom and so on. In the case of the Yogis, that nature does not change either in the past or in the future; it remains as it is. So also *svābhāvikī*, intrinsic—that which follows from the very nature of things, as for instance, such characteristics as heat or light in the case of fire etc. That nature also does not change according to place or time. Similarly, *sahajā*, instinctive, born with oneself, as for instance such activities of birds as flying in the sky. Any other behaviour, too, is natural, *yā akṛtā*, that is not produced by anything else, as for instance the tendency of water to flow down. And anything else, *yā na jahāti svabhāvam*, that does not change its character; *sā*, all that; *vijñeyā*, is to be known, in this world; as *prakṛtiḥ*, nature. The idea sought to be conveyed is this: When the nature of empirical things, that are falsely imagined, does not change itself, what need can there be to point out that the natural immortality of the intrinsically birthless ultimate realities, is not subject to mutation?

What constitutes that nature, whose change is assumed by the disputants? And what is the defect in such an assumption? The answer is this:

जरामरणनिर्मुक्ताः सर्वे धर्माः स्वभावतः ।
जरामरणमिच्छन्तश्च्यवन्ते तन्मनीषया ॥१०॥

10. All souls are intrinsically free from old age and death. But by imagining senility and death, and being engrossed in that thought, they deviate (from their nature).

Jarā-maraṇa-nirmuktāḥ, free from old age and death, i.e. free from all (physical) changes—*jarā*, old age, and (ending with) *maraṇa*, death, etc. Who are they? *Sarve dharmāḥ*. all entities, i.e. all the souls; *svabhāvataḥ*, by nature. Although the souls are intrinsically so, yet *icchantaḥ*, thinking, as though thinking, imagining; *jarāmaraṇam*, old age and death, for the Self, like the imagining of a snake on a rope; they *cyavante*, fall, that is so say, deviate, from their own nature; *tanmanīṣayā*, because of that thought—thought of senility and death, that is to say, because of the defect of being engrossed in that kind of thought.

The Vaiśeṣika points out how the Sāṁkhyas, holding the view of the pre-existence of the effect in the cause, talk illogically:

कारणं यस्य वै कार्यं कारणं तस्य जायते ।
जायमानं कथमजं भिन्नं नित्यं कथं च तत् ॥११॥

11. The cause must undergo birth according to one who holds that the cause itself is the effect. How can a thing be birthless that takes birth, and how can it be eternal when it can be subject to (partial) disintegration?

The disputant, *yasya*, according to whom; *kāraṇam*, the cause itself (existing) in the form of materials like earth; is the *kāryam*, effect, that is to say, evolves into the effect; *tasya*, from his point of view; *kāraṇam*, the cause, e.g. the Pradhāna (or Primordial Nature), though itself unborn; *jāyate*, undergoes birth, as the effects like Mahat and the rest. This is the idea. If Pradhāna is *jāyamānam*, born, as Mahat and the rest; *katham*, how, is it said by them; to be *ajam*, birthless? For it is a contradiction in terms to say that a thing is unborn and yet has birth. Moreover, they say that the Pradhāna is eternal. How can it be eternal if it is *bhinnam*, split up, disintegrated (transformed), partially? For a composite thing, a jar for instance, which is subject to partial disintegration, is not seen to be eternal in this world. This is the idea. The meaning sought to be imparted is that it involves a contradiction on their part to say that a thing may be broken up partially and yet be birthless and eternal.

For elucidating the same idea it is said:

कारणाद्यद्यनन्यत्वमतः कार्यमजं यदि ।
जायमानाद्धि वै कार्यात्कारणं ते कथं ध्रुवम् ॥१२॥

12. If (according to you) the effect be non-different from the cause, then on that account the effect, too, is birthless. And if that be so, how can your cause be still eternal, it being non-different from its effect which is subject to birth?

Yadi, if; it is your intention to hold that there is *ananyatvam*, non-difference, of the effect; *kāraṇāt*, from the cause, which is birthless; then from that it follows that *kāryam ajam*, the effect is birthless. This is a fresh contradiction in your view that a thing is a product and yet birthless. Besides, there is this additional contradiction: If the effect and the cause are non-different, *katham*, how; can *te*, your; *kāraṇam*, cause; which is non-different *kāryāt jāyamānāt*, from the effect that is subject to birth; be yet *dhruvam*, eternal? For one half of a hen cannot be cooked, while the other half is reserved for laying eggs.

There is this further consideration:

अजाद्वै जायते यस्य दृष्टान्तस्तस्य नास्ति वै ।
जाताच्च जायमानस्य न व्यवस्था प्रसज्यते ॥१३॥

13. That disputant has certainly no supporting illustration who holds that the effect is produced out of an unborn cause. If the produced effect is held to

be born out of another born thing, that, too, leads to no solution.

That disputant, *yasya*, according to whom; the effect *jāyate*, is produced; *ajāt*, from an unborn thing; *tasya*, for him; *na asti vai dṛṣṭāntaḥ*, there is absolutely no illustration (in support). The idea is that, in the absence of any supporting illustration, it stands proved by implication that nothing is born of the unborn. On the other hand, if it is held *jāyamānasya*, with regard to the produced effect; that it comes *jātāt*, from a born thing; then since the latter must come out of another born thing and the last one, again, from another born thing, *na vyavasthā prasajyate*, there will be no solution at all; or in other words it will lead to an infinite regress.

By the Vedic text, 'But when to the knower of Brahman everything has become the Self (then what should one know and throught what?)' (Bṛ. II. iv. 14), it has been said that from the highest standpoint there is no duality. Taking its stand on this, the (next) verse says:

हेतोरादिः फलं येषामादिर्हेतुः फलस्य च ।
हेतोः फलस्य चानादिः कथं तैरुपवर्ण्यते ॥१४॥

14. How can beginninglessness be declared for cause and effect by those (disputants) according to whom the effect is the origin of the cause and the cause the origin of the effect?

The disputants, *yeṣām*, according to whom; the *phalam*, effect, the aggregate of body and senses; is the *ādiḥ*, source; *hetoḥ*, of the cause, of merit etc.; and similarly, the *hetuḥ*, cause—merit etc.; is the *ādiḥ*, source; *phalasya*, of the effect, of the aggregate of body and senses—while thus positing a beginning for the cause and the effect by the very assertion that these are mutually the sources and products of each other[1]—*katham taiḥ upavarṇyate*, how can it be asserted by them; that the cause and effect are beginningless? In other words, this is self-contradictory, for the Self that is eternal and unchanging can neither become the cause nor the effect.

How do they make a contradictory assertion? That is being shown:

हेतोरादिः फलं येषामादिर्हेतुः फलस्य च।
तथा जन्म भवेत्तेषां पुत्राज्जन्म पितुर्यथा ॥१५॥

15. Just as a father may be born of a son, so also may birth be a possibility according to those (disputants) who admit that the effect is the source of the cause and the cause is the source of the effect.

Those who assert that the cause originates from the effect, which is itself produced by the cause, get involved in a contradiction that is on a par with that

[1] Merit and demerit result from embodiment; and embodiment results from merit and demerit.

implied in *pituḥ janma putrāt*, the birth of the father from a son.

If it be contended that the contradiction pointed out above cannot be reasonably advanced, we say,

संभवे हेतुफलयोरेषितव्यः क्रमस्त्वया ।
युगपत्संभवे यस्मादसंबन्धो विषाणवत् ॥१६॥

16. A sequence has to be found out by you in the births of cause and effect. For should they originate together, there can be no causal relation, as between the two horns of a cow.

Kramaḥ, a sequence — viz that the cause precedes and the effect succeeds; *eṣitavyaḥ*, has to be found out; *tvayā*, by you; *sambhave*, in the births; *hetu-phalayoḥ*, of cause and effect. This is necessary for this further reason: *Yasmāt*, since; *yugapat sambhave*, should there be a simultaneous origin, of the cause and effect; there will be *asambandhaḥ*, want of relationship, through causality, as in the case of the two horns of a cow growing together on the left and the right.

How will they be unrelated? That is being stated:

फलादुत्पद्यमानः सन्न ते हेतुः प्रसिध्यति ।
अप्रसिद्धः कथं हेतुः फलमुत्पादयिष्यति ॥१७॥

17. If your cause has to come out of an effect, it can have no right to recognition. How will a cause,

which is not established as such, produce a result?

Utpadyamānaḥ san, if it has to originate; *phalāt*, from an effect, which is still to be born, which is itself yet without any existence—which is non-existent like the horn of a hare; *hetuḥ*, the cause; *na prasidhyati*, has no right to recognition; it does not have any birth. *Katham*, how; your *hetuḥ*, cause; which is yet to be endued with substance; and *aprasiddhaḥ*, is not established as such, like the horn of a hare; *utpādayiṣyati phalam*, will produce a result? For it is not seen anywhere that two things that depend for existence on each other, and are analogous to the horns of a hare, are connected causally or in any other way. This is the idea.

यदि हेतोः फलात्सिद्धिः फलसिद्धिश्च हेतुतः ।
कतरत् पूर्वनिष्पन्नं यस्य सिद्धिरपेक्षया ॥१८॥

18. If the subsistence of the cause is dependent on the effect, and the subsistence of the effect is dependent on the cause, then which of the two has existence earlier, with relation to which the other may emerge?

If, even after the dismissal of any causal relation between the (so-called) cause and the (so-called) effect by pointing out the defect that they cannot be interrelated, it is still contended by you that the cause and the effect subsist by mutual interdependence, then tell me which one among the cause and the effect pre-exists, depending on the pre-existence of which the succeeding one may emerge into being. This is the idea.

अशक्तिरपरिज्ञानं क्रमकोपोऽथवा पुनः ।
एवं हि सर्वथा बुद्धैरजातिः परिदीपिता ॥१९॥

19. Your inability to answer this will amount to your ignorance, or there will be falsification of the sequence (asserted by you). Thus indeed is highlighted in every way the absence of birth by the learned ones.

On the other hand, if you think that you have no answer, then this *aśaktiḥ*, inability, of yours; will amount to (the fallacy of) *aparijñānam*, want of knowledge of reality, i.e. ignorance; *athavā*, or there will be; *kramakopaḥ*—*kopa*, reversal, falsification, of the *krama*, sequence, spoken of by you, consisting in mutual succession in the sense that the effect derives its subsistence from the cause, and the cause derives its subsistence from the effect. This is the meaning. *Evam*, thus, from the fact that any causal relation between the cause and the effect cannot be substantiated; *ajātiḥ*, the absence of birth, the non-origination of everything; *paridīpitā*, has been highlighted; *buddhaiḥ*, by the learned people, the disputants who speak of the defects of each other's point of view. This is the purport.

Objection: We spoke of the causal relation existing between the cause and the effect, whereas, playing merely on the words, you resorted to trickery saying that it is like the birth of the father from a son, that there is no such connection between the two like the two horns of a cow, and so on. Not that we asserted the production of an effect from a cause that did not exist, or the derivation of a cause from a non-existing effect. What did we say then? It was admitted by us that causality is the kind of relation existing between the seed and the sprout.

With regard to this the *answer* is:

बीजाङ्कुराख्यो दृष्टान्तः सदा साध्यसमो हि सः ।
न हि साध्यसमो हेतुः सिद्धौ साध्यस्य युज्यते ॥२०॥

20. What is known as the illustration of the seed and the sprout is ever on an equal footing with the (unproved) major term. For an illustration that is as unproved as the major term is not applied for establishing the relation of the major term with the minor term.

(This is but begging the question, because the supporting) *dṛṣṭāntaḥ*, illustration; that is *bījāṅkurākhyaḥ*, known as that of the seed and the sprout; is *sādhyasamaḥ*, on an equal footing with my major term (that has still to be proved). This is the idea.

Objection: Is it not a matter of experience that the causal relation between the seed and the sprout is without a beginning?

Answer: Not so, for it is admitted that the earlier ones have their beginning like the succeeding ones. Just as a separate sprout that has originated now from a seed has a beginning and another seed born out of a separate sprout has also a beginning by the very fact of succession in birth, similarly the antecedent sprouts as well as the antecedent seeds must have a beginning. And thus since each one of the whole chain of seeds and sprouts has a beginning, it is illogical to assert eternality for any one of them. So also is the case with regard to causes and effects. If now it is argued that the chain of causes and effects is without a beginning, we say, no; for any unity of such a series cannot be upheld. Indeed, apart from the causes and effects, even those who talk of the beginninglessness of such a series do not certainly vouch for a unitary entity called either a chain of seeds and sprouts or a procession of causes and effects. Therefore it has been well said, 'How can beginninglessness be declared by them for cause and effect?' (*Kārikā*, IV. 14). Thus since your view involves an illogicality from a fresh point of view, we are not really avoiding the point at issue. This is the idea. Moreover, *hetuḥ*, an illustration; that is *sādhyasamaḥ*, as unproved as the major term; is not applied by those who are adepts in the use of the valid means of proof (i.e. inference); *sādhyasiddhau*, in the matter of establishing a relation between the major term and the minor term (in a syllogism). This is the meaning. The 'illustration' is to be understood here by the term *hetuḥ* (lit. middle term), for an illustration substantiates the ground of inference; and what is under discussion is the illustration, and not the middle term.

It is being shown how birthlessness is highlighted by the wise:

पूर्वापरापरिज्ञानमजातेः परिदीपकम् ।
जायमानाद्धि वै धर्मात् कथं पूर्वं न गृह्यते ॥२१॥

21. The ignorance of the precedence and succession is a pointer to beginninglessness itself. For if it be a fact that a thing takes birth, why is not its cause apprehended?

And the fact that there is *pūrvāparāparijñānam*, ignorance of the precedence and succession, of the cause and the effect; that is *paridīpakam*, a pointer to, i.e. an indication of; *ajāteḥ*, birthlessness. If an entity takes birth, *katham*, why; is its *pūrvam*, antecedent cause; *na gṛhyate*, not grasped? By one who perceived a thing undergoing birth must also be perceived, as a matter of necessity, the originator of that thing; for the begetter and the begotten are inevitably inter-related. Therefore that is a pointer to birthlessness.

स्वतो वा परतो वाऽपि न किंचिद्वस्तु जायते ।
सदसत् सदसद्वाऽपि न किंचिद्वस्तु जायते ॥२२॥

22. A thing, whatsoever it may be, is born neither of itself, nor of something else, (nor of both together). Nothing whatsoever is born that (already) exists, does not exist, or both exists and does not exist.

For this further reason also nothing whatsoever that is *sat*, existing; *asat*, non-existing; or *sat-asat*, existing and non-existing, takes birth; since a thing that (supposedly) undergoes birth, *na jāyate*, is not born; *svataḥ*, of itself; *parataḥ*, of another; *vā*, or, of both. There is no possibility of birth for it in any way. To illustrate: As a jar does not come out of that very jar, so nothing, that has not itself come into existence, can be born *svataḥ*, out of its own form by itself. Nor does it take birth *parataḥ*, from another, as something different from that another, just as a cloth is not born of a pot or a cloth from another cloth. Similarly a thing is not born both out of itself and another, just as a jar or a cloth is not born out of a jar and a cloth, for this involves a contradiction.

Objection: Is not a jar produced from earth and a son born of a father?

Answer: True, the ignorant have such notions and use such words as 'It exists', 'It takes birth'. Those very words and notions are examined by the discriminating people as to whether they are true or false, inasmuch as things called a jar, a son, and so on, which are contents of words and notions, are found on examination to be reduced to mere words, as is declared in the Vedic text, '(All modification) has speech as its basis . . .' (Ch. VI. i. 4). If a thing already exists, then just because it exists, it does not pass into birth like earth or a father. If a thing does not exist, then by the very fact of non-existence it does not undergo birth like the horn of a hare etc. If it is both existent and non-existent, then also it does not take birth, as it is impossible to have a thing that is self-contradictory. Hence it is established that nothing whatsoever is born. As for those (Buddhists) who assert that a product is nothing more than the mere act of birth, and by whom it is held accordingly that actions, accessories, and results are but the same identical entity and that things are momentary, they are far out of the reaches of reasonableness, because (according to this theory) a thing cannot be apprehended as 'This is so', since it ceases to exist for a second moment immediately after being perceived, and because memory of a thing not perceived earlier becomes impossible.

Besides, by asserting that the cause and the effect are without beginning, you admit perforce that the cause and the effect are without birth. If you ask, 'How is it?', the answer is:

हेतुर्न जायतेऽनादेः फलं चापि स्वभावतः ।
आदिर्न विद्यते यस्य तस्य ह्यादिर्न विद्यते ॥२३॥

23. A cause is not born of a beginningless effect; nor does an effect naturally come out (of a beginningless cause). (Cause and effect are thus birthless) for a thing that has no cause, has certainly no birth.

Anādeḥ, from a beginningless, effect; *hetuḥ na jāyate*, the cause is not born. For you do not certainly mean that from a beginningless effect, which is not born, the cause derives its birth. Nor do you mean that the *phalam*, effect; also gets its birth *svabhāvataḥ*, naturally, without any reason; *anādeḥ*, from an unborn cause that is beginningless. Accordingly, you virtually admit the birthlessness of cause and effect by asserting that they have no beginning. *Hi*, for; in this world, *yasya*, anything for which; *ādiḥ*, a cause; *na vidyate*, does not exist; *tasya*, for that thing; *na vidyate*, cannot exist; *ādiḥ*, a beginning, the birth, mentioned earlier; because birth is admitted for a thing that has a cause, and not for a causeless one.

An *objection* is being raised again in order to emphasize what has already been said:

प्रज्ञप्तेः सनिमित्तत्वमन्यथा द्वयनाशतः।
संक्लेशस्योपलब्धेश्च परतन्त्रास्तिता मता॥२४॥

24. (We have to admit) that knowledge has its objects, since a contrary supposition leads to an annihilation of duality. And the existence of objects, as supported by the opposite systems of thought, is also admitted from the fact of the experience of pain.

Prajñapti means knowledge, perception of sound etc. That knowledge is possessed of a *nimitta*, cause, i.e. an object. So *sanimittatvam* means the fact that it has an object—it has objective reference apart from its own subjective existence. This is what we admit. Perception of sound and the rest cannot be contentless, for it is related to objects. *Anyathā*, otherwise (in the absence of objects); there would result a void, *dvayanāśataḥ*, as a consequence of the annihilation of duality—consisting in a variety of experiences of sound, touch, blueness, yellowness, redness, etc. This is the meaning. Nor can it be said that duality, consisting in a variety of experiences, does not exist, for this is a matter of direct perception. Accordingly, from the fact that duality—variety of experiences—is perceived, *paratantrāstitā*, existence as held by the scriptures of other schools, that is to say, existence of external objects, apart from their knowledge, as held by the books of opposite schools; *matā*, is admitted. For knowledge, which is of the nature of mere illumination, cannot have any variety amounting to a mere natural diversification within itself unless there is that variety in the corresponding objects, e.g. blueness, yellowness, etc., just as a crystal can have no variety unless it comes into relation with such limiting adjuncts as blueness etc. This is the idea. The external objects, as held by the opposite systems, have existence because of the further reason of *saṁkleśa*, lit. suffering, which is the same as *saṁkleśana*, causing of suffering; so it means pain. Pain arising from a burn etc. is a matter of experience. If, apart from knowledge, there were nothing externally present to cause a burn for instance, pain would not have been experienced. Therefore, from this fact, we admit that there is an external object. For there can be no pain in knowledge as such, since this is not the case elsewhere.[1]

As to this the *reply* (of the subjective-idealist) is:

प्रज्ञप्तेः सनिमित्तत्वमिष्यते युक्तिदर्शनात् ।
निमित्तस्यानिमित्तत्वमिष्यते भूतदर्शनात् ॥२५॥

25. In accord with the perception of its cause, knowledge is supposed to be based on external objects. But from the standpoint of reality, it is held that the external cause is no cause.

[1] E.g. where the body is not in actual contact with fire.

It is true that *yuktidarśanāt*, in compliance with the logic of the experience of duality and pain; *iṣyate*, it is thus posited, by you; that *sanimittatvam prajñapteḥ*, there is an external object for knowledge. Now hold fast to your logic that external objects are the basis of experience.

Opponent: Tell me what follows from that.

The *answer* is: By us *iṣyate*, it is held; that *nimittasya animittatvam*, the cause—a jar or anything else that is assumed to be the basis of experience—is no cause; it is not the basis, the cause, of variety.

Objection: Why?

Answer: *Bhūtadarśanāt*, from the standpoint of reality, that is to say, of the ultimate Reality. For, unlike the existence of a buffalo independently of a horse, a jar does not exist apart from clay after being recognized as clay that it really is, nor does a cloth exist apart from the yarns, nor the yarns apart from the fibres. Thus if the reality is pursued successively till words and notions cease, we do not perceive any external cause of knowledge at all. This is the meaning.

Or the phrase may be *abhūtadarśanāt* (and not *bhūtadarśanāt*) in which case the meaning is: *Abhūtadarśanāt*, on account of finding the external object to be unreal; *animittatvam iṣyate*, it is not admitted to be the cause (of knowledge), just as a snake seen on a rope is not. Besides, the cause is not a cause, since it is the content of an erroneous perception; and as such, it ceases to be so when the error is removed. For to the people in deep sleep, divine absorption (*samādhi*), or Liberation, where there is no erroneous perception, there is no knowledge of any external object, except (the consciousness of) the Self. Nor is a thing perceived by a madman perceived to be such by others who are in their senses. Hereby is demolished the arguments based on perception of duality and experience of pain.

चित्तं न संस्पृशत्यर्थं नार्थाभासं तथैव च।
अभूतो हि यतश्चार्थो नार्थाभासस्ततः पृथक् ॥२६॥

26. Consciousness has no contact with objects; so also it has certainly no contact with appearances of objects. For according to the reasons adduced, an object has no existence, and an illusory object is not separate from the awareness.[1]

As there is no external objects, therefore the *cittam*, consciousness; *na spṛśati*, does not come in contact with; *artham*, an object, anything acting externally as a support; nor does it come in contact with *arthābhāsam*, any appearance of an object, for it is as much a form of consciousness as the consciousness in dream; *hi*, for; *yataḥ*, in accordance with the above reasoning; *arthaḥ*, an object; is *abhūtaḥ*, non-existent, even in the

[1] We are dealing here with the Buddhist view. A.G. explains *citta* as *sphuraṇa*, Self-emanation, shining. The act of knowing implies an object to be known, but consciousness, thought of as shining like the sun, needs no object. Besides, the sun and its shining are the same, though in common parlance a distinction is made between them.

waking state, just as a dream object is. *Na*, nor even is; *arthābhāsaḥ*, an illusory object; *pṛthak*, different, from consciousness; it is consciousness alone that appears as objects like the jar etc. as it does in a dream.

Objection: In that case, the appearance of consciousness, in the form of a jar for instance even when there is no jar etc., must be a false perception. And if this be the conclusion, you should point out the (corresponding) right knowledge somewhere (so as to call this an error).

With regard to this, the *answer* (of the subjectivist) is:

निमित्तं न सदा चित्तं संस्पृशत्यध्वसु त्रिषु ।
अनिमित्तो विपर्यासः कथं तस्य भविष्यति ॥२७॥

27. Consciousness does not ever come in contact with external objects in all the three states. There being no external objects, how can there be any baseless, false apprehension of it?

Cittam, consciousness; *na sadā saṁspṛśati*, does not ever touch; any *nimittam*, cause, external object; *triṣu adhvasu*, in all the three states (of past, present, and future). Should it come in contact with any object at any time, that will be non-erroneous, i.e. the highest reality, and in relation to that true perception, the illusive perception of a jar, where there is no jar, will be a false perception. But there is no contact of consciousness with any object at any time. Therefore *katham*, how; *bhaviṣyati*, will there be; *tasya*, for that consciousness; *viparyāsaḥ animittaḥ*, any false apprehension that has no object to support it? The idea implied is that there is no such thing as false knowledge at all. Rather it is the nature of consciousness that even in the absence of jar etc. it appears like those things.[1]

The text starting with, 'In accord with the perception of its cause, knowledge . . .' (IV. 25) and ending with the previous verse, which represents the view of the subjective-idealists among the Buddhists, is approved by the teacher (Gauḍapāda) in so far as it refutes the view of those who believe in external objects. Now he makes use of that very argument (of the idealists) as a ground of inference for demolishing their own points of view:

तस्मान्न जायते चित्तं चित्तदृश्यं न जायते।
तस्य पश्यन्ति ये जातिं खे वै पश्यन्ति ते पदम् ॥२८॥

28. Hence consciousness has no birth, and things perceived by it do not pass into birth. Those who perceive the birth of that consciousness, may as well see footmarks in space itself.

[1] Those who in a case of illusion, hold the theory of *anyathākhyāti*, appearance of a real thing in a wrong way, believe that an illusion presupposes a true perception somewhere. But the subjective-idealists say that an error does not imply an earlier true knowledge, for an illusion and the objects in an illusion are all appearances of consciousness.

Since from the standpoint of reality, we also approve the view of the subjective-idealists that consciousness appears as a jar even though there is no such jar etc., therefore it also stands to reason that consciousness also appears to be born even though there is no such thing as birth. And therefore the *cittam*, consciousness; *na jāyate*, does not pass into birth; just as much as *cittadṛśyam na jāyate*, the things perceived by consciousness have no birth. Therefore *ye*, those, the idealists, who; *paśyanti*, perceive; the *jātim*, birth; *tasya*, of that consciousness, along with its momentariness, sorrowfulness, voidness, non-selfhood, etc. —thereby presuming to perceive through that very consciousness the nature of consciousness which defies all perception; *te*, they, those idealists; *paśyanti*, see; *padam*, the footprint, of birds etc.; *khe vai*, in space itself. That is to say, they are bolder even than the other dualists. As for the nihilists, who, while perceiving the non-existence of everything, assert thereby the voidness of their own philosophy, they are even bolder than the idealist,[1] inasmuch as they want to have the sky itself in their grasp.

Through the above reasons it is established that Brahman is one and has no birth. Now the present verse is meant for summing up, in the form of a result

[1] It is through perception that the all-round voidness is proved. But how will perception itself be annulled? Not that perception can annihilate itself, for the simple reason that perception and its negation cannot coexist. Besides, if you talk of absolute nihilism, you affirm the non-existence of your own view as well.

(of the discussion), what was presented in the beginning as a proposition:

अजातं जायते यस्मादजातिः प्रकृतिस्ततः ।
प्रकृतेरन्यथाभावो न कथंचिद्भविष्यति ॥२९॥

29. It is the birthless that (according to the disputants) takes birth. Since birthlessness is its very nature, therefore, the transmutation of (this) nature can take place in no way whatsoever.

Since it is imagined by the disputants that the unborn consciousness, which is nothing but Brahman, takes birth; therefore it is the *ajātam*, unborn; that *jāyate*, takes birth. *Yasmāt*, since; *ajātiḥ*, birthlessness; is its *prakṛtiḥ*, nature; *tataḥ*, therefore; *anyathābhāvaḥ*, transmutation, birth; *prakṛteḥ*, of that nature, which is essentially unborn; *na katham cit bhaviṣyati*, will not take place in any way.

Here is another loophole discovered in the view of those who hold that the worldly state (i.e. bondage) and Liberation of the soul are real:

अनादेरन्तवत्त्वं च संसारस्य न सेत्स्यति ।
अनन्तता चादिमतो मोक्षस्य न भविष्यति ॥३०॥

30. Moreover, if the world be beginningless, its termination will not be achieved. And there will be no eternality for Liberation that has a beginning.

Saṁsārasya anādeḥ, of the world (i.e. of bondage)

which has no beginning, no definite non-existence in the past; *antavattvam*, termination; *na setsyati*, cannot be established, on the basis of reasoning; for, in common experience, nothing is seen to have an end that has no beginning.

Objection: It is seen that the continuity of the serial relation between the seed and the sprout breaks (though it has no beginning).

Answer: Not so, for this was refuted by pointing out that a series does not constitute a single substance (*Kārikā*, IV. 20).

Similarly, *na bhaviṣyati*, there will be no; *anantatā*, everlastingness; even *mokṣasya*, of Liberation, that has a beginning, that originates at the time of attainment of illumination; for this is not seen in the case of jars etc.

Objection: Since like non-existence brought about by the destruction of a jar etc., Liberation, too, is not a substance, therefore our point of view is free from defect.[1]

Answer: On that assumption[2] your proposition that Liberation has existence from the standpoint of ultimate Reality will fall through. Besides, it will have no beginning just because it will be non-existent like the horn of a hare.

[1] Non-existence brought about by destruction has a beginning but no end, and non-existence is not a substance just as much as Liberation is not.

[2] If Liberation is non-existence.

आदावन्ते च यन्नास्ति वर्तमानेऽपि तत्तथा।
वितथैः सदृशाः सन्तोऽवितथा इव लक्षिताः ॥३१॥

31. That which does not exist in the beginning and the end, is equally so in the middle. Though they are similar to the unreal, yet they are seen as though real.

सप्रयोजनता तेषां स्वप्ने विप्रतिपद्यते।
तस्मादाद्यन्तवत्त्वेन मिथ्यैव खलु ते स्मृताः ॥३२॥

32. Their utility is contradicted in dream. Therefore from the fact of their having a beginning and an end, they are rightly held to be unreal.

These two verses, which were explained in the chapter 'On Unreality' (*Kārikā*, II. 6-7), are quoted here in connection with the non-existence of bondage and Liberation.

सर्वे धर्मा मृषा स्वप्ने कायस्यान्तर्निदर्शनात्।
संवृतेऽस्मिन् प्रदेशे वै भूतानां दर्शनं कुतः ॥३३॥

33. All entities are unreal in dream, since they are seen within the body. How can there be the vision of creatures within this narrow space here?[1]

[1] In this way the verse indirectly aims at proving the falsity of all. If falsity in dream follows from the fact that things are seen inside the body, then all things even in the waking state must be false, since they are seen within the body of Virāṭ. And if falsity

The topic raised in, 'But from the standpoint of reality, it is held that the external cause is no cause' (*Kārikā*, IV. 25), is being elaborated by these verses.

न युक्तं दर्शनं गत्वा कालस्यानियमाद्गतौ ।
प्रतिबुद्धश्च वै सर्वस्तस्मिन् देशे न विद्यते ॥३४॥

34. It is not proper to hold that dream objects are experienced by reaching them, since the requisite time involved in the journey is lacking. Moreover, nobody, on waking up, continues in the place of dream.

The idea implied is that there is no going over to any other place in dream, for the time required for and the distance involved in coming and going, as validly settled in the waking state, *aniyamāt*, have no corresponding fixity, in the dream state.

मित्राद्यैः सह संमन्त्र्य संबुद्धो न प्रपद्यते ।
गृहीतं चापि यत्किंचित्प्रतिबुद्धो न पश्यति ॥३५॥

35. Having conferred with friends and others (in dream) one does not get confirmation when awake. And whatever one acquired in dream, one does not see it after waking up.

---

of dream objects follows from the fact of their being seen within a place that is not adequate for them, then things of the waking state must be false since they, though naturally associated with space and time, are still seen in Brahman that has no space and time—A.G.

Saṁmantrya, having deliberated; *mitrādyaiḥ saha*, with friends and others (in dream); one *na prapadyate*, does not get confirmation, of that very deliberation; when *pratibuddhaḥ*, up from dream. And *yat kim cit*, whatever, gold etc.; *gṛhītam*, was acquired; he does not get after waking.[1] For this reason, too, one does not go to a different place in dream.

स्वप्ने चावस्तुकः कायः पृथगन्यस्य दर्शनात् ।
यथा कायस्तथा सर्वं चित्तदृश्यमवस्तुकम् ॥३६॥

36. Moreover the body (seen) in a dream is unsubstantial, since another body is seen (to exist). As it is the case with the body, so is everything perceived through consciousness and is (therefore) unsubstantial.

And the *kāyaḥ*, body; that is seen *svapne*, in dream, to be walking about; is *avastukaḥ*, unsubstantial; *anyasya pṛthak darśanāt*, since another (sleeping) body, as distinguished from the one in the state of dream, is seen separately. The idea is this: As the body seen in dream is unreal, so all things seen through consciousness even in the waking state are unreal, for they are all equally perceived through consciousness. The significance of the topic under discussion is that the waking state also is unreal, since it is similar to the dream state.

[1] An alternative meaning is: To the man of illumination (*pratibuddhaḥ*) there is no consciousness of anything except Brahman. So what may appear to others as his eating, drinking, etc., does not appear to himself to be so, for he thinks, 'I do not do anything' (G. V. 8)—A.G.

Things of the waking state are unreal because of this further reason:

ग्रहणाज्जागरितवत्तद्धेतुः स्वप्न इष्यते ।
तद्धेतुत्वात्तु तस्यैव सज्जागरितमिष्यते ॥३७॥

37. Since a dream is experienced like the waking state, the former is held to be the result of the latter. In reality, however, the waking state is admitted to be true for that dreamer alone, it being the cause of his dream.

Grahaṇāt, since dream is experienced; *jāgaritavat*, like the waking state, as characterized by the subject-object relationship; therefore dream *iṣyate*, is held; *taddhetuḥ*, as having that waking state as its source; that is to say, dream is a product of the waking state. *Taddhetutvāt*, since dream has that waking state as its cause; that *jāgaritam*, waking state; is *sat*, true; *tasya eva*, for that dreamer alone; but not so for the others, just like the dream itself. This is the implication. As a dream is true to a dreamer alone, so far as it appears like objects of common experience having existence, similarly the waking things that appear like existing objects of common experience are true to the dreamer alone, since (according to him) they are the cause of his dream. In reality, however, just like dream objects, the things of the waking state, too, are not objects of common experience to all, (nor have they existence). This is the purport.

Objection: Even though the objects of the waking

state be the prototypes of those of the dream state, they are not unsubstantial like dream; for dream is extremely changeful, whereas the waking state is seen to be steady.

Answer: This is truly so to the non-discriminating people, but to the man of discrimination nothing whatsoever is known to have origination. Therefore—

उत्पादस्याप्रसिद्धत्वादजं सर्वमुदाहृतम् ।
न च भूतादभूतस्य संभवोऽस्ति कथंचन ॥३८॥

38. Since origination is not a well-established fact, it is declared (by the Upaniṣads) that everything is birthless. Moreover, there is no origination, in any way whatsoever, of any non-existing thing from an existing one.

Utpādasya aprasiddhatvāt, as origination is not a well-established fact; so in the text, 'co-extensive with everything within and without, and since He is birthless' (Mu. II. i. 2), it has been *udāhṛtam*, declared, by the Upaniṣad in effect; that *sarvam ajam*, everything is birthless; or in other words, the (birthless) Self is everything. And your further conjecture that the unreal dream originates from the real waking state is also untenable. For in this world *na asti saṁbhavaḥ abhūtasya*, there is no origination of a nonentity; *bhūtāt*, from a real thing; for a nonentity, like the horn of a hare, is not seen to originate in any way whatsoever.

Objection: Has it not been said by yourself that

dream is a product of the waking state? So how is it said that origination is not a well-recognized fact?

Answer: As to that, listen to what we mean by the causal relation (between them):

असज्जागरिते दृष्ट्वा स्वप्ने पश्यति तन्मयः ।
असत्स्वप्नेऽपि दृष्ट्वा च प्रतिबुद्धो न पश्यति ॥३९॥

39. Having seen some unreal thing in the waking state and being emotionally affected, one sees it in dream also. And having even seen some unreal thing in dream, one does not see it in the waking state.

Dṛṣṭvā, having seen; *jāgarite*, in the waking state; *asat*, an unreal, illusory thing, like a snake imagined on a rope; and becoming *tanmayaḥ*, emotionally affected by its thoughts; one *paśyati*, sees; *svapne*, in dream, also, by imagining the duality of subject and object as in the waking state. Similarly, unless one resorts to imagination, one, *dṛṣṭvā*, after having seen; *asat*, an unreal thing; *svapne api*, even in dream; *na paśyati*, does not see (it); *pratibuddhaḥ*, when he is awake. From the use of the word '*ca*, and', it follows that, in a similar way, one does not sometimes see in dream something that one had seen in the waking state. In this sense the waking state is said to be the cause of dream, but thereby it is not implied that the former is real.

In reality, however, it cannot be established that anything has any causal relationship with something in any way whatsoever. How?

नास्त्यसद्धेतुकमसत्सदसद्धेतुकं तथा ।
सच्च सद्धेतुकं नास्ति सद्धेतुकमसत्कुतः ॥४०॥

40. There is no unreal thing that has an unreality as its cause; similarly there is no unreal thing that has a reality as its cause. Moreover, there is no existing thing that has another existing thing as its cause. How can there be an unreal thing that is produced out of something real?

Na asti asat, there is no unreal thing; *asaddhetukam*, that has an unreal thing for its cause—e.g. an unreal thing like a flower in the air that has an unreal thing like a hare's horn as its cause. Similarly, *na asti sat*, there is no such existing entity, a jar for instance; that is *asaddhetukam*, the product of an unreality—a hare's horn for instance. *Tathā*, so also; *na asti sat*, there is no existing thing, a pot for instance, that is a product of another existing thing, a jar for instance. How can there be any possibility of an unreality being produced out of a reality? Besides, there is no other kind of causal relationship possible or imaginable. So the idea implied is that, to the discriminating people, causal relationship of anything whatsoever is really an unestablished fact.

Again, by way of removing any surmise about the causal relationship between the unreal waking and dream states, it is said:

विपर्यासाद्यथा जाग्रदचिन्त्यान् भूतवत् स्पृशेत् ।
तथा स्वप्ने विपर्यासाद्धर्मांस्तत्रैव पश्यति ॥४१॥

41. As some one, owing to lack of discrimination, may in the waking state, be in contact with unthinkable objects, fancying them to be real, so also in dream, one sees the objects in that dream alone, owing to want of discrimination.

Yathā, as; some one, *viparyāsāt*, owing to want of discrimination; may imagine *jāgrat*, in the waking state; as though one is in touch with *acintyān*, unthinkable objects, like a snake etc. imagined on a rope etc.; *bhūtavat*, as if they were real; *tathā*, so also; *svapne*, in dream; *viparyāsāt*, owing to want of discrimination; he fancies as though visualizing *dharmān*, objects, like elephants etc., that is to say, he sees them there in the dream alone, and not as the products of the waking state.

उपलम्भात्समाचारादस्तिवस्तुत्ववादिनाम् ।
जातिस्तु देशिता बुद्धैरजातेस्त्रसतां सदा ॥४२॥

42. Instruction about creation has been imparted by the wise for the sake of those who, from the facts of experience and adequate behaviour, vouch for the existence of substantiality, and who are ever afraid of the birthless entity.

For those who *upalambhāt*, because of perception; and *samācārāt*, adequate behaviour, e.g. proper observance of duties pertaining to castes and stages of life —(i.e.) for those who, because of these two reasons, *astivastutvavādinām*, resort to the declaration of existence of substantiality—for the sake of those who are earnest in their effort, who are faithful, but who are possessed of an inferior kind of discrimination; that *jātiḥ*, birth (creation); *deśitā*, has been inculcated—as a means to the attainment of the Reality; *buddhaiḥ*, by the wise, by the non-dualists, with the idea: 'Let them accept it for the time being. But in the case of those practising Vedānta, the discriminating knowledge about the birthless and non-dual Self will arise in them spontaneously.' But they have not done so from the standpoint of the ultimate Truth. And this is so because those non-discriminating people (for whom such instruction is meant) are devoted to Vedic conduct, while, owing to their dull intellect, they are *sadā*, ever; afraid, *ajāteḥ*, of the birthless entity; apprehending that this will lead to their annihilation. This is the idea. It was said earlier, 'that is merely by way of generating the idea (of oneness)' (*Kārikā*, III. 15).

अजातेस्त्रसतां तेषामुपलम्भाद्वियन्ति ये ।
जातिदोषा न सेत्स्यन्ति दोषोऽप्यल्पो भविष्यति ॥४३॥

43. For those who, being afraid of the Unborn, deviate from the true path by relying on their experience of duality, the faults arising from acceptance of creation will not bear fruit; and the fault, too, will be insignificant.

And *ye*, those who; thus, *upalambhāt*, relying on perception, as well as adequate behaviour; and *ajāteḥ trasatām*, being afraid of the unborn entity (i.e. the Self); and declaring that duality exists, *viyanti*, deviate, from the non-dual Self, that is to say, accept duality—

(i.e.) in the case of the people who are afraid of the Unborn, but are faithful, and tread the righteous path, *jātidoṣāḥ*, the faults arising from the perception of origination; *na setsyanti*, will not attain fruition, for they are treading the path of discrimination. *Doṣāḥ api*, should there be any *doṣāḥ*, defect, caused by non-attainment of full enlightenment; that *api*, too; *alpaḥ bhaviṣyati*, will be insignificant.

Objection: As perception and adequate behaviour are valid proofs, things comprised in duality do exist.

Answer: Not so, for perception and adequate behaviour are not universally true. How they are not universally true is being shown:

उपलम्भात्समाचारान्मायाहस्ती यथोच्यते ।
उपलम्भात्समाचारादस्ति वस्तु तथोच्यते ॥४४॥

44. As an elephant conjured up by magic is called an elephant by depending on perception and adequate behaviour, so from the facts of perception and adequate behaviour a thing is said to be existing.

As *māyāhastī*, an illusory elephant conjured up by magic, though non-existent in reality, is yet certainly perceived, just like a real elephant—people behave towards it in this world just as with a real elephant, and call it an elephant because of such characteristics of an elephant as being capable of being bound, ridden upon, etc.; similarly *upalambhāt samācārāt*, because of perception and appropriate conduct (with regard to them); *ucyate vastu asti*, it is said that duality, consisting of diversity, does exist. Therefore the purport is that the facts of being perceived and dealt with appropriately cannot be the tests establishing the existence of a thing.

What, again, is the absolutely real thing which is the substratum of all unreal ideas of creation and the rest? The answer is:

जात्याभासं चलाभासं वस्त्वाभासं तथैव च ।
अजाचलमवस्तुत्वं विज्ञानं शान्तमद्वयम् ॥४५॥

45. It is Consciousness—birthless, motionless and non-material, as well as tranquil and non-dual—which has the semblance of birth, appears to move, and simulates a substance (possessed of qualities).

That which being birthless has the semblance of birth is *jātyābhāsam*, as for instance in the illustration, 'Devadatta has birth'. That which appears as though moving is *calābhāsam*, as in the case, 'That very Devadatta goes'. *Vastu* is a substance that can have attributes; that which simulates that is *vastvābhāsam*, as for instance in the illustration, 'That very Devadatta is fair or tall'. Devadatta appears as though taking birth, as though he moves, and as if he is fair or tall, though in reality he is birthless, changeless, and non-material. What is it that answers to these characteristics? It is *vijñānam*, Consciousness. It is *śāntam*, quiescent, being devoid of birth etc. And therefore It is also *advayam*, without a second. This is the meaning.

एवं न जायते चित्तमेवं धर्मा अजाः स्मृताः।
एवमेव विजानन्तो न पतन्ति विपर्यये ॥४६॥

46. Thus Consciousness has no birth; thus are the souls considered to be birthless. Those who know thus indeed, do not fall into calamity.

Evam, thus, in accordance with the reasons adduced; *cittam na jāyate*, Consciousness[1] does not undergo birth; *evam*, thus; are *dharmāḥ*, the souls; *smṛtāḥ*, considered—by the knowers of Brahman; to be *ajāḥ*, birthless. The plural in *dharmāḥ* (souls) is used metaphorically, since the non-dual Self Itself appears to be different in accordance with the multiplicity of bodies. Those who, after renouncing all cravings for external things, *vijānantaḥ evam eva*, know this indeed, that the aforesaid Consciousness, free from birth etc., is the non-dual reality which is the Self; *na patanti*, do not fall again; *viparyaye*, into calamity, into the sea of the darkness of ignorance, as is confirmed by the text of the Vedic verse, 'what delusion and what sorrow can there be for that seer of oneness?' (Īś. 7).

In order to dilate upon the above-mentioned realization of the Self, the text goes on:

ऋजुवक्रादिकाभासमलातस्पन्दितं यथा।
ग्रहणग्राहकाभासं विज्ञानस्पन्दितं तथा ॥४७॥

47. As the movement of a firebrand appears to

[1] '*Citta* means Consciousness, i.e. Brahman.'—A.G.

be straight or crooked, so is it the vibration of Consciousness that appears to be the knower and the known.

Yathā, as; in common experience, it is seen that *alātaspanditam*, the movement of a firebrand; *ṛjuvakrādikābhāsam*, appears to be straight, curved and so on; *tathā*, similar; is *grahaṇagrāhakābhāsam*, the appearance as the perception and the perceiver, that is to say, as the object and the subject. What is it that appears? *Vijñānaspanditam*, the vibration of Consciousness, as it were, it being set in motion by ignorance, for the unmoving Consciousness can have no vibration, as it was indeed said earlier, 'birthless, motionless' (*Kārikā*, IV. 45).

अस्पन्दमानमलातमनाभासमजं यथा ।
अस्पन्दमानं विज्ञानमनाभासमजं तथा ॥४८॥

48. As the firebrand, when not in motion, becomes free from appearances and birth, so Consciousness, when not in vibration, will be free from appearances and birth.

Yathā, as; that very *alātam*, firebrand; *aspandamānam*, when not in motion, when it does not undergo birth to become straight etc. in shape; it remains *anābhāsam ajam*, free from appearances and birth; *tathā*, so; Consciousness, which vibrates through ignorance, will, on the cessation of ignorance, become *aspandamānam*, free from vibration, consisting in birth etc.—will remain free from appearances, birth, and vibration. This is the meaning.

Moreover,

अलाते स्पन्दमाने वै नाभासा अन्यतोभुवः ।
न ततोऽन्यत्र निस्पन्दान्नालातं प्रविशन्ति ते ॥४९॥

49. When the firebrand is in motion, the appearances do not come to it from anywhere else. Neither do they go anywhere else from the firebrand when it is at rest, nor do they (then) enter into it.

Alāte spandamāne, when that very firebrand is in motion; the appearances of straightness, crookedness, etc. do not come to be in it, *anyataḥ*, from anywhere outside the firebrand; this is what is meant by *na anyatobhuvaḥ*, non-adventitious. *Na*, nor; do they go out anywhere else, *tataḥ nispandāt*, from that firebrand, when it is at rest. *Na te alātam praviśanti*, nor do they enter into the motionless firebrand itself.

Furthermore,

न निर्गता अलातात्ते द्रव्यत्वाभावयोगतः ।
विज्ञानेऽपि तथैव स्युराभासस्याविशेषतः ॥५०॥

50. They did not issue out of the firebrand, by reason of their unsubstantiality. With regard to Consciousness also the appearances must be of a similar kind, for as an appearance there is no distinction.

Te, they, the appearances; *na nirgatāḥ alātāt*, do not issue out of the firebrand, like something out of a house; *dravyatva-abhāva-yogataḥ*, because of their being devoid of substantiality, that is to say, because of unsubstantiality, the phrase being construed thus: The quality of a *dravya*, substance, is *dravyatva*; the absence of that is *dravyatvābhāva*; and *yogataḥ* means by reason of. Entry is possible for things and not for those that are not so. The appearances of birth etc., *vijñāne api tathaiva syuḥ*, in Consciousness also must be thus alone; *ābhāsasya aviśeṣataḥ*, for as an appearance there is no distinction.

It is being shown how they are similar:

विज्ञाने स्पन्दमाने वै नाभासा अन्यतोभुवः ।
न ततोऽन्यत्र निस्पन्दान्न विज्ञानं विशन्ति ते ॥५१॥
न निर्गतास्ते विज्ञानाद् द्रव्यत्वाभावयोगतः ।
कार्यकारणताऽभावाद्यतोऽचिन्त्याः सदैव ते ॥५२॥

51. When Consciousness is in vibration, the appearances do not come to It from anywhere else. Neither do they go anywhere else from Consciousness when It is at rest, nor do they (then) enter into It.

52. They did not issue out of Consciousness, by reason of their unsubstantiality; for they are ever beyond comprehension, being without any relation of cause and effect (with Consciousness).

Everything with regard to Consciousness is similar to that of the firebrand; Consciousness has this one distinction that It is ever unmoving. It is being pointed out as to what causes the appearances of creation etc. in the motionless Consciousness: *Yataḥ*, for; *te*, they; are *sadā eva acintyāḥ*, ever beyond comprehension; *kāryakāraṇatā-abhāvāt*, in consequence of the absence of any logical connection of cause and effect (between the appearances and Consciousness), they being of the nature of non-existence. Just as the ideas of straightness etc. are perceived in the firebrand itself, although the appearances of straightness etc. are unreal, similarly the ideas of creation etc. in the absolute Self, which appear even though there are no creation etc., must be false. This is the purport as a whole (of the two verses).

It has been established that the Reality which is the Self, is one and unborn. Now, according to those who imagine causality,

द्रव्यं द्रव्यस्य हेतुः स्यादन्यदन्यस्य चैव हि।
द्रव्यत्वमन्यभावो वा धर्माणां नोपपद्यते ॥५३॥

53. A substance can be the cause of a substance, and one thing can be the cause of another different from itself. But the souls can be considered neither as substances nor as something different from other things.

Dravyam, a substance; *syāt hetuḥ*, can be the cause; *dravyasya*, of a substance; *anyat anyasya*, one thing can be the cause of another; but a thing cannot be its own cause. Nor is a non-substance seen in common experience to be independently a cause of anything.[1] *Na upapadyate*, nor is it logical, in anyway whatsoever; that *dharmāṇām dravyatvam anyabhāvaḥ vā*, the souls should be considered either as substances or as something different from other things, under which possibility alone could the Self become either a cause or an effect.[2] Thus since the Self is neither a substance nor different from anything,[3] It is neither the cause nor the effect of anything. This is the meaning.

एवं न चित्तजा धर्माश्चित्तं वाऽपि न धर्मजम् ।
एवं हेतुफलाजातिं प्रविशन्ति मनीषिणः ॥५४॥

54. In this way the external entities are not the products of Consciousness; nor is Consciousness a product of external entities. Thus the wise confirm the birthlessness of cause and effect.

Evam, thus, according to the reasons adduced; Consciousness is the very essence of the Self that is identical with Consciousness. Hence *dharmāḥ*, external entities; *na cittajāḥ*, are not the products of Consciousness;[4] *na cittam dharmajam*, nor is Consciousness a product of external entities. For all entities are the mere appearances of that which is essentially Consciousness. Consequently, an effect is not produced

[1] Quality, action, genus, etc. can be causes through the substances in which they inhere.
[2] For causality presupposes difference.
[3] I.e. the Self being all-pervasive and homogeneous.
[4] A.G. equates *citta* with the supreme Self.

from a cause, nor is a cause from an effect. In this way the knowers of Brahman, *praviśanti*, enter into, affirm; *hetuphalājātim*, the birthlessness of cause and effect. The idea is that they arrive at the non-existence of cause and effect.

It is being pointed out as to what will happen to those, again, who cling to cause and effect:

यावद्धेतुफलावेशस्तावद्धेतुफलोद्भवः ।
क्षीणे हेतुफलावेशे नास्ति हेतुफलोद्भवः ॥५५॥

55. Cause and effect spring into being so long as there is mental preoccupation with cause and effect. There is no origination of cause and effect when the engrossment with cause and effect becomes attenuated.

Yāvat, as long as; *hetuphalāveśaḥ*, attention is riveted on cause and effect, under the idea, 'I am the producer of the causes called virtue and vice; merit and demerit belong to me; and I shall enjoy their fruit by being born sometime and somewhere among the host of creatures'—as long as causality is superimposed on the Self, as long as the mind is preoccupied with it; *tāvat hetuphalodbhavaḥ*, so long do cause and effect, merit and demerit and their effect, arise, i.e. are active without a break. When the engrossment with cause and effect, which springs from ignorance, is removed through the realization of non-duality as stated before, like the removal of the possession by evil spirit through the power of incantation and medicines, then that engrossment *kṣīṇe*, being attenuated; *na asti hetuphalodbhavaḥ*, there is no origination of cause and effect.

What is the harm even if there is the origin of cause and effect? The answer is:

यावद्धेतुफलावेशः संसारस्तावदायतः।
क्षीणे हेतुफलावेशे संसारं न प्रपद्यते ॥५६॥

56. As long as there is mental preoccupation with causality, so long does the worldly state continue. When engrossment with causality is exhausted, one does not attain the worldly state.

Yāvat, as long as, mental preoccupation with causality is not removed through perfect illumination; *tāvat*, so long; *saṁsāraḥ*, the worldly state; persisting unimpaired, remains *āyataḥ*, outstretched, that is to say, continues for long. But, again, *hetuphalāveśe kṣīṇe*, when engrossment with causality is attenuated; *na prapadyate saṁsāram*, one does not attain the worldly state; for then there is no cause for it.

Objection: As there is nothing else apart from the unborn Self, how can it be said by you that there are such phenomena as the origin and destruction of cause and effect as well as of the world?

Answer: Listen:

संवृत्या जायते सर्वं शाश्वतं नास्ति तेन वै।
सद्भावेन ह्यजं सर्वमुच्छेदस्तेन नास्ति वै ॥५७॥

57. Everything seems to be born because of the empirical outlook; therefore there is nothing that is eternal. From the standpoint of Reality, everything is the birthless Self; therefore there is no such thing as annihilation.

Sarvam jāyate, everything is produced; *saṁvṛtyā*, by *saṁvaraṇa*, concealment, consisting in the empirical outlook within the domain of ignorance. *Tena*, therefore; within the range of ignorance, *na asti vai śāśvatam*, there is surely nothing that is eternal. Hence it has been said that the world, characterized by origin and destruction, remains outstretched. But, *sadbhāvena*, from the standpoint of the highest Reality; since *sarvam ajam*, everything is the birthless Self; *tena*, therefore; in the absence of birth, *na asti vai*, there is surely no; *ucchedaḥ*, annihilation, of any cause, effect, etc. This is the meaning.

धर्मा य इति जायन्ते जायन्ते ते न तत्त्वतः ।
जन्म मायोपमं तेषां सा च माया न विद्यते ॥५८॥

58. The entities that are born thus are not born in reality. Their birth is as that of a thing through Māyā (magic). And that Māyā again has no reality.

Ye dharmāḥ, the entities, souls and other things, which; *jāyante*, are born, are imagined to be born; *te*, they; that are *iti*, of this kind—the word '*iti*, of this kind' indicates the empirical outlook mentioned earlier (IV. 57); so the meaning is, 'The entities, that are of this kind, are born thus owing to (concealment through) the empirical outlook'; *te*, they; *na jāyante*, are not born; *tattvataḥ*, in reality. And as for the *janma*, creation—owing to the concealment (the empirical outlook); *teṣām*, of those—of those entities mentioned above; that birth is to be understood *māyopamam*, like what occurs through Māyā (magic). It is to be understood as similar to magic.

Objection: Then there is an entity called Māyā.

Answer: Not so. *Sā ca māyā na vidyate*, and that Māyā does not exist; the idea being that the term Māyā relates to something non-existing.

It is being shown how their birth can be compared to magical birth:

यथा मायामयाद् बीजाज्जायते तन्मयोऽङ्कुरः।
नासौ नित्यो न चोच्छेदी तद्वद्धर्मेषु योजना ॥५९॥

59. As from a magical seed grows a sprout equally illusory—it being neither eternal nor destructible—just so is the logic (of birth or death) applicable in the case of objects.

Yathā, as; *māyāmayāt bījāt*, from a magical seed, of a mango for instance; *jāyate*, grows; *aṅkuraḥ tanmayaḥ*, a sprout (of equal substance), equally illusory; *asau*, that one, the sprout; being *na nityaḥ*, neither eternal; *na ca ucchedī*, nor destructible—simply because it has no existence; *tadvat*, just so; is the *yojanā*, reasoning; about birth and death, *dharmeṣu*, in the case of the objects. The idea is that, from the standpoint of Reality, there can be no real birth or death for the objects.

नाजेषु सर्वधर्मेषु शाश्वताशाश्वताभिधा ।
यत्र वर्णा न वर्तन्ते विवेकस्तत्र नोच्यते ॥६०॥

60. With regard to all the birthless entities there can be no application of the words 'eternal' and 'non-eternal'. No categorical statement can be made with regard to an entity where words do not apply.

But from the standpoint of absolute Truth, *śāśvatā-śāśatābhidhā*, the terms 'eternal' or 'non-eternal'; *na ajeṣu dharmeṣu*, do not apply to the birthless entities, the souls, whose essence consists in a mere eternal and homogeneous Consciousness. This is the meaning. The term *varṇāḥ* derivatively signifies those by which things are described and it means words. *Yatra*, where, with regard to which (souls), words do not apply, so far as their description or revelation is concerned; *tatra*, there; *na ucyate*, is not uttered; any *vivekaḥ*, categorical statement, that 'This is so indeed', or in other words that 'It is either eternal or non-eternal', as is declared in the Vedic text, 'From where speech returns' (Tai. II. iv. 1).

यथा स्वप्ने द्वयाभासं चित्तं चलति मायया ।
तथा जाग्रद्द्वयाभासं चित्तं चलति मायया ॥६१॥

अद्वयं च द्वयाभासं चित्तं स्वप्ने न संशयः ।
अद्वयं च द्वयाभासं तथा जाग्रन्न संशयः ॥६२॥

61. As in dream Consciousness (*cittam*) vibrates as though having dual functions, so in the waking state Consciousness vibrates as though with two facets.

62. There is no doubt that Consciousness, though one, appears in dream in dual aspects; so also in the waking state, Consciousness, though one, appears to have two aspects.

That the absolute Consciousness, which is really non-dual, becomes an object of speech, is due only to the activities of mind, but not so in reality. The verses were explained earlier[1] (*Kārikā*, III. 29-30).

For this further reason, duality, describable by words, does not exist:

स्वप्नदृक्प्रचरन् स्वप्ने दिक्षु वै दशसु स्थितान् ।
अण्डजान् स्वेदजान् वाऽपि जीवान्पश्यति यान् सदा ॥६३॥
स्वप्नदृक्चित्तदृश्यास्ते न विद्यन्ते ततः पृथक् ।
तथा तद्दृश्यमेवेदं स्वप्नदृक्चित्तमिष्यते ॥६४॥

63-64. The creatures—be they born from eggs or from moisture—which the experiencer of dream ever sees as existing in all the ten directions, while he is roaming in the dreamland, are but objects of perception to the consciousness of the dreamer, and

[1] The word *manaḥ* occurring in *Kārikā*, III.29–30, is substituted here by *cittam* (meaning Consciousness in the Vedāntic, and not in the Buddhistic sense). In verses 64–67, *citta* means empirical consciousness.

they do not exist apart from that consciousness. Similarly, this consciousness of the dreamer, is admitted to be only an object of perception to that dreamer.

Yān jīvān, the creatures which; the *svapnadṛk*, seer of a dream; *sadā paśyati*, ever sees; *svapne caran*, while moving in dream, in the place seen in a dream; *dikṣu vai daśasu sthitān*, as existing in all the ten directions; be they *aṇḍajān*, those born from eggs; or *svedajān*, those born from moisture.

Objection: If that be so, what follows therefrom?

The *answer* is: *Te*, those creatures; are the *svapnadṛkcittadṛśyāḥ*, objects of perception to the consciousness of the experiencer of dream. Therefore *na vidyante*, they do not exist; *tataḥ pṛthak*, separately from the consciousness of the dreamer. This is the idea. It is consciousness alone that is imagined in the forms of diverse objects like creatures etc. *Tathā*, similarly; even *idam*, this; which is *svapnadṛkcittam*, the consciousness of the experiencer of dream; is *idam taddṛśyam eva*, merely an object of perception to that dreamer. *Tad-dṛśyam* means the experience (*dṛśyam*) of that (*tat*) dreamer. Therefore, such a thing as consciousness has no existence apart from the dreamer. This is the idea.

चरञ्जागरिते जाग्रद्दिक्षु वै दशसु स्थितान् ।
अण्डजान् स्वेदजान् वाऽपि जीवान्पश्यति यान्सदा ॥६५॥

जाग्रच्चित्तेक्षणीयास्ते न विद्यन्ते ततः पृथक् ।
तथा तद्दृश्यमेवेदं जाग्रतश्चित्तमिष्यते ॥६६॥

65-66. The creatures—be they born from eggs or from moisture—which the experiencer of the waking state ever sees as existing in all the ten directions, while he is roaming in the places of the waking state, are but objects of perception to the consciousness of the man in the waking state, and they do not exist separately from that consciousness. Similarly, this consciousness of the waking man is admitted to be only an object of perception to the waking man.

The creatures visible to a waking man are non-different from his consciousness, since they are perceived through consciousness, just like the creatures perceived by the consciousness of a dreamer. And that consciousness, again, engaged in the perception of creatures, is non-different from the experiencer, since it is perceived by the experiencer, like the consciousness in the dream state. The remaining portion has already been explained.

उभे ह्यन्योन्यदृश्ये ते किं तदस्तीति नोच्यते।
लक्षणाशून्यमुभयं तन्मतेनैव गृह्यते ॥६७॥

67. They are both perceptible to each other. (If the question arises), 'Does it exist?' the answer given is, 'No'. Both of them lack valid proof, and each is perceived merely because of a prepossession with the other.

Te ubhe, both of them—consciousness and the creatures—knowledge and its modifications—these two; are *anyonyadṛśye*, objects of perception to each other. For the thing that is called knowledge is what it is in relation to its objects such as the creatures; and the objects of perception, such as the creatures, are so in relation to knowledge; consequently, their awareness is mutually determined. Hence, when it is asked, '*Kim tat asti iti*, does it exist?'; *ucyate*, the answer made, by the discriminating man is, '*na*, no'—nothing whatsoever, be it knowledge or the things perceived through knowledge, exists. For in dream neither an elephant nor a knowledge having an elephant as its content exists. So also, in the waking state, these do not exist according to the discriminating people. This is the idea implied. How? Since *ubhayam*, both, knowledge and the objects of knowledge; are *lakṣaṇāśūnyam*, devoid of *lakṣaṇā*, anything whereby they can be established; that is to say, they are both without valid proof. Either is *gṛhyate*, perceived; *tanmatena eva*, merely because of a prepossession with the other. There can be no knowledge of the pot by setting aside the idea of the pot, nor can there be any comprehension of the idea of the pot by discarding the pot. The meaning implied is that in the case under discussion no distinction, of one being the knowledge and the other its object, can be made between the two.

यथा स्वप्नमयो जीवो जायते म्रियतेऽपि च।
तथा जीवा अमी सर्वे भवन्ति न भवन्ति च॥६८॥

68. As a creature seen in a dream undergoes birth and death, so also do all these creatures appear and disappear.

यथा मायामयो जीवो जायते म्रियतेऽपि च।
तथा जीवा अमी सर्वे भवन्ति न भवन्ति च ॥६९॥

69. As a creature conjured up by magic undergoes birth and death, so also do all these creatures appear and disappear.

यथा निर्मितको जीवो जायते म्रियतेऽपि वा।
तथा जीवा अमी सर्वे भवन्ति न भवन्ति च ॥७०॥

70. As a creature produced through medicines and charms undergoes birth and death, so also do all these creatures appear and disappear.

Māyāmayaḥ means one that is created by a magician; and *nirmitakaḥ* means created by medicines, charms, etc. As egg-born creatures and others, created in dreams or by magic and incantation, take birth and die, so also do such creatures as human beings who are verily non-existent and are merely imagined on Consciousness. This is the idea.

न कश्चिज्जायते जीवः संभवोऽस्य न विद्यते।
एतत्तदुत्तमं सत्यं यत्र किंचिन्न जायते ॥७१॥

71. No creature whichsoever has birth, there is no source for it. This is that highest truth where nothing whatsoever is born.

It has been said that birth, death, etc. of creatures within the range of empirical existence are like those of the creatures in dream etc.; but the highest truth is that where no creature undergoes birth. The remaining portion was explained before (*Kārikā*, III. 48).

चित्तस्पन्दितमेवेदं ग्राह्यग्राहकवद्द्वयम् ।
चित्तं निर्विषयं नित्यमसङ्गं तेन कीर्तितम् ॥७२॥

72. This duality, possessed of subject and object, is a mere vibration of Consciousness. And Consciousness is objectless; hence It is declared to be eternally without relations.

All *dvayam*, duality; *grāhya-grāhakavat*, possessed of subject and object; is *cittaspanditam eva*, surely a vibration of Consciousness. But from the ultimate standpoint, *cittam*, Consciousness, is nothing but the Self; and accordingly it is *nirviṣayam*, without objects. *Tena*, as a consequence of that, because of Its being without objects; It is *kīrtitam*, declared; to be *nityam asaṅgam*, ever without relations, as is known from the Vedic text, 'For this infinite being is unattached' (Bṛ. IV. iii. 15-16). Anything that has its objects becomes connected with those objects. As Consciousness is objectless, It is unrelated. This is the purport.

Objection: If the unrelatedness of Consciousness follows from the fact of Its being without objects, then there can be no freedom from relation, since there exist such objects as the teacher, the scripture, and the taught.

Answer: That is no defect.

Objection: Why?

The *answer* is:

योऽस्ति कल्पितसंवृत्या परमार्थेन नास्त्यसौ।
परतन्त्राभिसंवृत्या स्यान्नास्ति परमार्थतः ॥७३॥

73. That which exists because of a fancied empirical outlook, does not do so from the standpoint of absolute Reality. Anything that may exist on the strength of the empirical outlook, engendered by other systems of thought, does not really exist.

An object, a scripture for instance, *yaḥ*, which; exists *kalpitasaṁvṛtyā*, because of a fancied empirical outlook (i.e. on the strength of empirical experience)—it being called so because it is an empirical outlook (*saṁvṛti*) that is imagined (*kalpita*) as a means for the attainment of the highest object; anything that exists by virtue of this, *asau na asti*, that has no existence; *paramārthena*, from the standpoint of the absolute Reality. It was said earlier, 'Duality ceases to exist after realization' (*Kārikā*, I. 18). And anything that *syāt*, may exist; *paratantrābhisaṁvṛtyā*, on the strength of the empirical outlook engendered by other systems of thought; that thing *paramārthataḥ*, when considered from the standpoint of the highest Reality; *na asti*, does not exist, to be sure. Therefore it has been well said, 'Hence it is declared to be without relations' (*Kārikā*, IV. 72).

Objection: On the assumption that scriptures etc.

have only empirical existence, the idea itself that something is birthless will be equally empirical.

Answer: Truly so.

अजः कल्पितसंवृत्या परमार्थेन नाप्यजः ।
परतन्त्राभिनिष्पत्त्या संवृत्या जायते तु सः ॥७४॥

74. Since in accordance with the conclusion arrived at in the scriptures of the other schools, the soul undergoes birth from the empirical point of view, therefore in pursuance of that fancied empirical view (it is said by the non-dualists that) the soul is birthless; but from the standpoint of absolute Reality, it is not even birthless.

Kalpitasaṁvṛtyā, in accordance with the empirical outlook, fostered with the help of scriptures etc.; the Self is said to be *ajaḥ*, unborn. But *paramārthena*, from the standpoint of the highest Reality; *na api ajaḥ*, It is not even unborn. For what is birthless *paratantrābhiniṣpattyā*, from the standpoint of the conclusions arrived at by other schools of thought; (is said to be so because) *saḥ*, that thing; *jāyate*, undergoes birth; *saṁvṛtyā*, as a matter of empirical experience. Therefore, even the imagination that the Self is birthless does not pertain to the absolutely real Entity. This is the idea.

अभूताभिनिवेशोऽस्ति द्वयं तत्र न विद्यते ।
द्वयाभावं स बुद्ध्वैव निर्निमित्तो न जायते ॥७५॥

75. There is in evidence a (mere) craving for false objects, (though) no duality is in existence there. Realizing the non-existence of duality, one becomes free from craving for false things, and one does not undergo birth.

Abhiniveśaḥ means mere strong attachment. Since no object exists, therefore there is in evidence a mere persistent infatuation for a non-existent duality. *Dvayam na vidyate tatra*, duality does not exist there. Since fondness for the unreal is alone the cause of birth, therefore *saḥ*, he; *na jāyate*, does not undergo birth; who *buddhvā*, having realized; *dvayābhāvam*, the non-existence of duality; has become *nirnimittaḥ*, free from cause, divested of the craving for the unreal duality.

यदा न लभते हेतूनुत्तमाधममध्यमान् ।
तदा न जायते चित्तं हेत्वभावे फलं कुतः ॥७६॥

76. When one does not perceive the superior, medium, and inferior causes, then Consciousness ceases to have births. For how can there be any result when there is no cause?

The highest causes are those duties which are enjoined in relation to castes and stages of life, which are performed by people free from hankering for results, which lead to the attainment of the states of gods and others, and which are purely virtuous. Those that are mixed with irreligious practices and lead to birth among men etc., are the middling ones. And the inferior causes are those particular tendencies that are known as irreligious and lead to birth among animals etc.. *Yadā*, when, after the realization of the reality of the Self which is one without a second and free from all imagination; one *na labhate*, does not perceive; all those causes — superior, intermediate, or inferior — that are fancied through ignorance, just as the dirt seen in the sky by children is not perceived there by a discriminating man; *tadā*, then; *cittam*, Consciousness; *na jāyate*, is not born, in the shape of gods and others that constitute the superior, medium, and inferior results. For when there is no cause, no effect can be produced just as no corn will grow unless there are seeds.

It has been firmly asserted that Consciousness has no birth in the absence of causes. Now is being stated in what, again, that birthlessness of Consciousness consists:

अनिमित्तस्य चित्तस्य याऽनुत्पत्तिः समाऽद्वया ।
अजातस्यैव सर्वस्य चित्तदृश्यं हि तद्यतः ॥७७॥

77. The birthlessness that Consciousness attains when freed from causes is constant and absolute; for all this (viz duality and birth) was perceptible to Consciousness that had been birthless and non-dual (even before).

Anutpattiḥ, the birthlessness, called Liberation, which comes; *cittasya animittasya*, to Consciousness that is causeless, that has become free from all the causes of birth called virtue and vice, as a consequence of the realization of the ultimate Truth—the birthlessness that is of this kind is for ever and under all circumstances *samā*, constant, without any distinction; and *advayā*, absolute. And this state *ajātasya*, belongs to the birthless, to Consciousness that had been birthless even before; (it belongs) *sarvasya*, (to Consciousness) that had been all, that is to say, to the non-dual Consciousness. Since even before the rise of knowledge, *tat*, all that—viz duality and birth; was *cittadṛśyam*, an object of perception to Consciousness; therefore the causelessness of the unborn non-dual Consciousness is ever the same and absolute, not that sometimes it is subject to birth and sometimes not. It is ever of the same nature. This is the meaning.

बुद्ध्वाऽनिमित्ततां सत्यां हेतुं पृथगनाप्नुवन् ।
वीतशोकं तथाऽकाममभयं पदमश्नुते ॥७८॥

78. After realizing causelessness as the truth, and not accepting any separate cause, one attains the state of fearlessness that is free from sorrow and devoid of desire.

Since duality, the cause of birth, does not exist in accordance with the reasons adduced, one *aśnute*, attains; the *abhayam padam*, state of fearlessness, which is free from desire, sorrow, etc. and is without ignorance etc.; that is to say, one is never reborn, *buddhvā*, after having realized; *animittatām satyām*, causelessness as the truth, of the highest order; and *anāpnuvan*, (after) not getting, that is to say, not accepting; any *pṛthak*, separate; *hetum*, cause, such as virtue etc., which may lead to birth among the gods and others—(that is to say), after having renounced the desire for all external things.

अभूताभिनिवेशाद्धि सदृशे तत्प्रवर्तते।
वस्त्वभावं स बुद्ध्वैव निःसङ्गं विनिवर्तते ॥७९॥

79. Since owing to a belief in the existence of unrealities, Consciousness engages Itself in things that are equally so (i.e. unreal), therefore when one has the realization of the absence of objects, Consciousness becomes unattached and turns back.

Abhūtābhiniveśaḥ consists in a conviction that duality does exist, even though there is no such thing. Since from this infatuation, which is a kind of delusion created by ignorance, *tat*, that Consciousness, which imitates the unreal; *pravartate*, engages; *sadṛśe*, in a similar thing; therefore when *saḥ*, anyone; realizes the non-existence of objects within duality, his Consciousness becomes *niḥsaṅgam*, unattached to it; and It *vinivartate*, turns back, from the objects that are the contents of the belief in the unreal.

निवृत्तस्याप्रवृत्तस्य निश्चला हि तदा स्थितिः।
विषयः स हि बुद्धानां तत्साम्यमजमद्वयम् ॥८०॥

80. For then, to the Consciousness which has got detached and does not engage (in duality), there follows the state of inactivity. Since that is the object realized by the wise, therefore that is the real equipoise, and that is birthless and non-dual.

Of the Consciousness *nivṛttasya*, that has desisted, from objects of duality; and *apravṛttasya*, does not engage in any other object because of the realization of the absence of any such thing; there follows *niścalā sthitiḥ*, a state of motionlessness, which is the very nature of Brahman. *Hi*, since; *saḥ viṣayaḥ*, that is the object of vision—this state of continuance of knowledge as Brahman that is a non-dual mass of homogeneous Consciousness; *buddhānām*, to the wise, who realize the supreme Reality; therefore, *tat*, that state; is the highest *sāmyam*, equipoise, without any differentiation; and it is also *ajam advayam*, birthless and non-dual.

It is again being shown what is the nature of the object of vision of the wise:

अजमनिद्रमस्वप्नं प्रभातं भवति स्वयम् ।
सकृद्विभातो ह्येवैष धर्मो धातुस्वभावतः ॥८१॥

81. This becomes birthless, sleepless, dreamless, and self-luminous. For this Entity is ever effulgent by Its very nature.

That becomes *prabhātam svayam*, fully illuminated by Itself, and It does not depend on the sun etc.; in other words, It is by nature self-effulgent. *Eṣaḥ*, this; *dharmaḥ*, entity, called the Self, that is possessed of such characteristics; is *sakṛt-vibhātaḥ*, always shining, that is to say, ever effulgent; *dhātusvabhāvataḥ*, by the very nature of the thing (that is the Self).

It is being shown why this supreme Reality, though spoken of thus, is not grasped by ordinary people:

सुखमाव्रियते नित्यं दुःखं विव्रियते सदा ।
यस्य कस्य च धर्मस्य ग्रहेण भगवानसौ ॥८२॥

82. Because of the passion for any object, whatever it be, that Lord becomes ever covered up easily, and He is at all times uncovered with difficulty.

Since *asau bhagavān*, that Lord, the non-dual Self, that is to say, the Deity; *sukham āvriyate*, is easily covered; *graheṇa yasya kasya ca dharmasya*, by the eagerness to grasp, because of the false belief in the reality of an object, whatever it be, that lies within duality—for the covering follows from the perception of duality, and it does not require any additional effort; and since It is *vivriyate*, uncovered, revealed; *duḥkham*, with difficulty, the knowledge of the supreme Reality being a rarity; therefore It is not easy to be understood, even though spoken of by the Upaniṣads and the teachers in various ways, as is pointed out by the Vedic text, 'the teacher is wonderful, and the receiver is wonderful' (Ka. I. ii. 7).

When the passionate attachment of the learned to even such subtle ideas as the existence of the Self or Its non-existence becomes a covering of the Lord, the supreme Self, what wonder is there that the passion in the shape of the intellectual preoccupation of the dull should be much more so? The next verse goes on to show this:

अस्ति नास्त्यस्ति नास्तीति नास्ति नास्तीति वा पुनः ।
चलस्थिरोभयाभावैरावृणोत्येव बालिशः ॥८३॥

83. By asserting that the Self 'exists', 'does not exist', 'exists and does not exist', or again, 'does not exist, does not exist', the non-discriminating man does certainly cover It up through ideas of changeability, unchangeability, both changeability and unchangeability, and non-existence.

Some disputant accepts the idea that the Self *asti*, exists. Another, viz the believer in momentariness of things, avers *na asti*, It does not exist. Another half-believer in momentariness, the naked one (i.e. Jaina) who speaks of both existence and non-existence, asserts, *asti na asti*, It exists and does not exist. The absolute nihilist says, *na asti*, *na asti*, It does not exist, It does not exist. Of these states, that of existence is *calaḥ*, changeable, it being different from such impermanent things as a jar;[1] and the state of non-existence is *sthiraḥ*, changeless, it being ever constant.[2] The state of both existence and non-existence is *ubhayam*, of either kind, since it relates to both the changeable and the changeless.[3] And *abhāvaḥ* relates to an absolute

[1] An object of perception is inconstant; the perceiving soul is different from it and reacts to it diversely, being, according to Nyāya-Vaiśeṣika, sometimes happy and sometimes sorry with regard to the same object.

[2] According to those who deny the existence of a perceiver apart from the intellect etc., the denial remains constant, for non-existence is changeless.

[3] The view of the Jainas.

non-existence.[1] *Bāliśaḥ* means a fool, a non-discriminating man. Each one of the fools, whether calling the Self existing or not, *eva*, surely; *āvṛṇoti*, covers up, the Lord; *calasthira-ubhaya-abhāvaiḥ*, by ideas of changeability, unchangeability, both changeability and unchangeability, and non-existence — which all belong to the four alternatives. The idea implied is that when even a learned man who has not realized the supreme Truth is but a fool, nothing need be spoken of one who is naturally stupid.

Of what nature, then, is the supreme Reality, by knowing which one gets rid of stupidity and becomes enlightened? The answer is:

कोटचश्चतस्र एतास्तु ग्रहैर्यासां सदाऽऽवृतः।
भगवानाभिरस्पृष्टो येन दृष्टः स सर्वदृक् ॥८४॥

84. These are the four alternative theories, through a passion for which the Lord remains ever hidden. He who sees the Lord as untouched by these is omniscient.

Etāḥ catasraḥ koṭyaḥ, these are the four alternative theories, viz 'It exists', 'It does not exist', and so on, which have been already mentioned and which are the conclusions arrived at by the scriptures of the dogmatic disputants; *grahaiḥ yāsām*, through the acceptance, through the conviction arising from the

[1] The view of the nihilistic Buddhists.

realization, of which alternatives; *bhagavān*, the Lord; remains *sadā āvṛtaḥ*, ever covered, to those sophists alone. *Saḥ*, he, the reflective sage; *yena*, by whom; *dṛṣṭaḥ*, has been realized; that Lord who, though remaining covered to the sophists, is really *aspṛṣṭaḥ ābhiḥ*, untouched by these—these four alternative theories of existence, non-existence, etc.; he who has realized the all-pervasive Being found and presented in the Upaniṣads alone, *saḥ*, that sage; is *sarvadṛk*, omniscient; or to put it otherwise, he is the truly enlightened man.

प्राप्य सर्वज्ञतां कृत्स्नां ब्राह्मण्यं पदमद्वयम् ।
अनापन्नादिमध्यान्तं किमतः परमीहते ॥८५॥

85. Does one make any effort after having attained omniscience in its fullness and having reached the non-dual state of Brāhmaṇahood, which has no beginning, middle, and end?

Prāpya, having attained; *sarvajñatām kṛtsnām*, omniscience in its fullness; and having reached the *brāhmaṇyam padam*, state of Brāhmaṇahood, as indicated in the Vedic texts, 'He (who departs from this world after knowing this immutable Brahman) is a Brāhmaṇa (i.e. a knower of Brahman)' (Bṛ. III. viii. 10), 'This is the eternal glory of a Brāhmaṇa (i.e. a knower of Brahman): (it neither increases nor decreases through work)' (Bṛ. IV. iv. 23); which non-dual state of Brāhmaṇahood, *anāpannādimadhyāntam*, has no beginning, middle, and end—that is to say, is devoid of origin, continuance, and dissolution; *kim īhate*, does one make any effort; *ataḥ param*, after this, after this attainment of the Self? The idea is that any effort becomes useless—in accordance with the Smṛti text, 'He has no end to achieve here either through activity or through inactivity' (G. III. 18).

विप्राणां विनयो ह्येष शमः प्राकृत उच्यते ।
दमः प्रकृतिदान्तत्वादेवं विद्वाञ्शमं व्रजेत् ॥८६॥

86. This is the modesty of the Brāhmaṇas, this is called their natural tranquillity, and this is their natural self-restraint resulting from spontaneous poise. Having known thus, one gets established in tranquillity.

This continuance in the state of identity with the Self is the natural *vinayaḥ*, modesty; *viprāṇām*, of the Brāhmaṇas. This is their humility, and this is also *ucyate*, called; their *prākṛtaḥ śamaḥ*, natural mental tranquillity. *Damah*, self-restraint, too, is this only; *prakṛtidāntatvāt*, because of (their) spontaneous poise, and because Brahman, too, is by nature quiescent. *Evam vidvān*, having known thus, having known the aforesaid Brahman as naturally tranquil; *vrajet*, one should attain; *śamam*, tranquillity, which is spontaneous and which is the very nature of Brahman—that is to say one remains established in identification with Brahman.

Thus since the philosophies of the sophists are at conflict with one another they lead to the worldly state, and they are the hot-houses for such drawbacks as attraction and repulsion. Accordingly, they are false philosophies. After having proved this fact by their own logic, the conclusion arrived at was that, being free from all the four alternatives, the most perfect philosophy is the naturally tranquil philosophy of non-duality which does not engender such faults as attachment etc. Now the following text starts to show our own process of arriving at truth:

सवस्तु सोपलम्भं च द्वयं लौकिकमिष्यते।
अवस्तु सोपलम्भं च शुद्धं लौकिकमिष्यते ॥८७॥

87. The ordinary (waking) state is admitted to be that duality, co-existing with things of empirical reality and fit to be experienced. The objectless ordinary (dream) state is admitted to be without any object and yet as though full of experience.

Savastu, empirical existence, is that which co-exists with an empirically real thing; similarly *sopalambham* is that which co-exists with experience. That is *dvayam*, duality, that is the source of all behaviour, scriptural and other, and that is characterized by the subject-object relationship. It is *laukikam*, the ordinary state, or in other words, the state of waking. In the Upaniṣads, the waking state is *iṣyate*, admitted, to be of such characteristics. That which is *avastu*, unsubstantial, there being an absence of empirical existence as well; which is *sopalambham*, associated with experience of things, as it were, though in fact there are no objects — that is *iṣyate*, admitted in the dream state; to be *śuddham*, pure, objectless, subtler[1] than the gross objects of the waking state; and it is *laukikam*, ordinary, being common to all beings.

अवस्त्वनुपलम्भं च लोकोत्तरमिति स्मृतम्।
ज्ञानं ज्ञेयं च विज्ञेयं सदा बुद्धैः प्रकीर्तितम् ॥८८॥

88. It is traditionally held that the extraordinary is without content and without experience. Knowledge, object, and the realizable thing are for ever declared by the wise.

That which is *avastu*, unsubstantial; *ca*, and; *anupalambham*, without experience, or in other words, that which is devoid of object and perception; is *smṛtam*, traditionally held to be; *lokottaram*, beyond the ordinary, and therefore, since it is devoid of those (objects and perception), it is super-normal; for the ordinary consists of objects and perception. The idea is that the state of deep sleep is the seed of all activity. That (mental state) is called *jñānam*, knowledge, by which is known in succession the supreme Reality together with Its means (of realization), the ordinary, the objectless ordinary, and the extraordinary. The *jñeyam*, object of knowledge, is comprised of all these three states, for logically there is no object (of knowledge) over and above these, the objects fancied by all the sophists being verily included in them. *Vijñeyam*, the object of realization, is the supreme Reality which

[1] Another reading is '*pravibhaktam*, different from'.

is called the Fourth, that is to say, the non-dual and birthless Reality that is the Self. All this, ranging from the ordinary to the realizable thing, *prakīrtitam*, is declared; *sadā*, for ever; *buddhaiḥ*, by the wise, by the seers of the *summum bonum*, by the knowers of Brahman.

ज्ञाने च त्रिविधे ज्ञेये क्रमेण विदिते स्वयम् ।
सर्वज्ञता हि सर्वत्र भवतीह महाधियः ॥८९॥

89. When after the acquisition of the knowledge (of the threefold object) and the knowledge of the objects in succession, the supreme Reality becomes self-revealed, then there emerges here, for the man of supreme intellect, the state of being All and enlightened for ever.

Jñāne (*vidite*), when (after) knowledge—knowledge of the ordinary etc.—is acquired; and *jñeye trividhe kramena* (*vidite*), when (after) the knowable things of three kinds are known in succession—viz first the gross ordinary, then when these are not present, the objectless ordinary, and in the absence of that again, the extraordinary; and then, when the three states are eliminated and the supreme Reality, the Fourth, the non-dual, birthless, and fearless *vidite*, has become known; *svayam*, of Its own accord; then *mahādhiyaḥ*, for the man of great intellect, for such a knower; *bhavati*, there emerges; *iha*, here, in this world; *sarva-jñatā*, the state of being All and enlightened; *sarvatra*, for ever, since his realization relates to what transcends the whole universe; that is to say, if one's true nature is realized once, it never leaves him. For unlike the knowledge of the sophists, there is no rise or decline of the knowledge of a man who has realized the highest Truth.

From the fact that the ordinary state etc. have been presented as objects to be known successively, some one may conclude that they have real existence. Hence it is said:

हेयज्ञेयाप्यपाक्यानि विज्ञेयान्यग्रयाणतः ।
तेषामन्यत्र विज्ञेयादुपलम्भस्त्रिषु स्मृतः ॥९०॥

90. Things to be rejected, realized, accepted, and made ineffective are to be known at the very beginning. From among them, the three, excepting the realizable, are traditionally held to be only fancies resulting from ignorance.

The *heya*, rejectable, are the three states counting from the ordinary. That is to say, just like the denial of an illusory snake on the rope, waking, dream, and sound sleep are to be denied as having any existence in the Self. The *jñeya*, thing to be known (realized), in this context, is the supreme Reality, free from the four alternatives (*Kārikā*, IV. 83). The *āpya*, acceptable, are the disciplines, called scholarship, the strength arising from knowledge, and meditativeness,[1] that

[1] Bṛ. III. v. 1: 'Therefore the knower of Brahman, having known all about scholarship, should try to live upon the strength which comes of knowledge; having known all about this strength as well as scholarship, he becomes meditative.'

are to be accepted by the monk after discarding the three kinds of desire (for progeny, property, and worlds). *Pākyāni*, those that are fit to be rendered ineffective—the blemishes, viz attraction, repulsion, delusion, etc., called passions (*kāṣāyas*). All these, viz those that are to be rejected, known, accepted, and rendered ineffective, are to be *vijñeyāni*, known well, by the monk; *agrayāṇataḥ*, in the beginning as (his) means. *Teṣām*, among those, among the things to be rejected etc.; *smṛtaḥ*, it is held traditionally, by the knowers of Brahman; that *vijñeyāt anyatra*, apart from Brahman alone which is to be realized, which is the ultimate Reality; there is *upalambhaḥ*, a mere imagination of perception, owing to ignorance, with regard to all the three—the rejectable, the acceptable, and the fit to be made ineffective. The idea is that those three are not admitted to be true from the highest standpoint.

But from the ultimate standpoint:

प्रकृत्याऽऽकाशवज्ज्ञेयाः सर्वे धर्मा अनादयः ।
विद्यते न हि नानात्वं तेषां क्वचन किंचन ॥९१॥

91. All the souls should be known as naturally analogous to space and as eternal. There is no plurality among them anywhere, even by a jot or tittle.

Sarve dharmāḥ, all the souls; *jñeyāḥ*, are to be known, by those who hanker after liberation; to be *prakṛtyā*, by nature; *ākāśavat*, analogous to space, in point of subtleness, freedom from taints, and all-pervasiveness; and (to be) *anādayaḥ*, eternal. Lest any misconception of diversity be created by the use of the plural number, the text says by way of rebutting it: *nānātvam*, plurality; *na vidyate*, does not exist; *teṣām*, among them; *kvacana*, anywhere; *kim cana*, even by a jot or tittle.

As for the souls being objects of cognition, that, too, is merely from empirical experience but not in Reality. This is being stated:

आदिबुद्धाः प्रकृत्यैव सर्वे धर्माः सुनिश्चिताः ।
यस्यैवं भवति क्षान्तिः सोऽमृतत्वाय कल्पते ॥९२॥

92. All the souls are, by their very nature, illumined from the very beginning, and their characteristics are well determined. He, to whom ensues in this way the freedom from the need of any further acquisition of knowledge, becomes fit for immortality.

Since just like the ever effulgent sun, *sarve dharmāḥ*, all the souls; are *prakṛtyā eva*, by their very nature; *ādibuddhāḥ*, illumined from the very beginning; that is to say, as the sun is ever shining, so are they ever of the nature of Consciousness, (therefore) there is no need for ascertaining their character; or in other words, their nature is ever well established, and it is not subject to such doubts as to 'whether it is so or not so'. As the sun is ever independent of any other light, for its own sake or for any other, so *yasya*, he, for whom, for which seeker after Liberation; *bhavati*, there occurs, in his own soul; *kṣāntiḥ*, eternal freedom from any need of further acquisition of knowledge—

either for himself or for others; *evam*, thus, in the way described above; *saḥ*, that man; *kalpate*, becomes fit; *amṛtatvāya*, for immortality; that is to say, he becomes able to attain Liberation.

Similarly, there is no need for bringing about tranquillity in the Self. This is being pointed out:

आदिशान्ता ह्यनुत्पन्नाः प्रकृत्यैव सुनिर्वृताः ।
सर्वे धर्माः समाभिन्नाः अजं साम्यं विशारदम् ॥९३॥

93. Since the souls are, from the very beginning tranquil, unborn, and by their very nature completely unattached, equal, and non-different, and since Reality is (thus) birthless, uniform, and holy, (therefore there is no need for any acquisition etc.).

Since *sarve dharmāḥ*, all the souls; are *ādiśāntāḥ*, tranquil from the beginning, always peaceful; and *anutpannāḥ*, birthless; *prakṛtyā eva sunirvṛtāḥ*, completely detached, by their very nature; *sama-abhinnāḥ*, equal and non-different; and since the reality of the Self is *ajam*, birthless; *sāmyam*, equipoised (uniform); *viśāradam*, holy; therefore there is no such thing as peace or Liberation that has to be brought about. This is the idea. For anything done can have no meaning for one that is ever of the same nature.

Those who have grasped the ultimate Truth, as described, are the only people in the world who are not pitiable; but the others are to be pitied. This is being stated:

वैशारद्यं तु वै नास्ति भेदे विचरतां सदा।
भेदनिम्नाः पृथग्वादास्तस्मात्ते कृपणाः स्मृताः ॥९४॥

94. There can be no perfection for people who have proclivity for multiplicity, tread for ever the path of duality, and talk of plurality. Hence they are traditionally held to be pitiable.

Since they are *bhedanimnāḥ*, have a proclivity for duality, follow duality, that is to say, confine themselves to the world—who are they? *Pṛthagvādāḥ*, those who talk of multiplicity of things, or in other words, the dualists—*tasmāt*, therefore; they are *smṛtāḥ*, traditionally held to be; *kṛpaṇāḥ*, pitiable. For, *na asti*, there is no; *vaiśāradyam*, perfection; *teṣām sadā vicaratām bhede*, for those who are ever roaming about in duality, that is to say, for those who ever persist in the path of duality conjured up by ignorance. Consequently, it is proper that they should be objects of pity. This is the purport.

The next verse says that this nature of the supreme Truth is beyond the ken of those who have not the requisite expansion of heart, who are not learned, who are outside the pale of Vedānta, who are narrow-minded, and who are dull of intellect.

अजे साम्ये तु ये केचिद्भविष्यन्ति सुनिश्चिताः।
ते हि लोके महाज्ञानास्तच्च लोको न गाहते ॥९५॥

95. They alone will be possessed of unsurpassable knowledge in this world, who will be firm in their

conviction with regard to That which is birthless and uniform. But the ordinary man cannot grasp That (Reality).

Ye kecit, those—even women and others, who perchance; *bhaviṣyanti*, will become; *suniścitāḥ*, firm in conviction, that 'This is so indeed'; with regard to the nature of the ultimate Reality, *aje sāmye*, which is birthless and uniform; *te hi loke mahājñānāḥ*, they alone in this world are possessed of great wisdom, or in other words, endowed with unsurpassing knowledge about the Reality. *Ca na lokaḥ*, and nobody, no other man of ordinary intellect; *gāhate*, can dip into, that is to say, grasp; *tat*, that thing, viz their path, the content of their knowledge—the nature of the ultimate Reality. For it is stated in the Smṛti, 'As it is not possible to sketch the flight of birds in the sky, so even the gods get puzzled in trying to trace the course of one who has become identified with the Self of all beings, who is a source of bliss to all, and who has no goal to reach' (Mbh. Śā. 239. 23-24).

The next verse says in what their great knowledge consists:

अजेष्वजमसंक्रान्तं धर्मेषु ज्ञानमिष्यते।
यतो न क्रमते ज्ञानमसङ्गं तेन कीर्तितम् ॥९६॥

96. It is traditionally held that the knowledge inhering in the birthless souls is unborn and non-relational. Since the knowledge has no objective relation, it is said to be unattached.

Since *iṣyate*, it is traditionally held; that the *jñānam*, knowledge; *ajeṣu dharmeṣu*, inhering in the birthless, steady, souls; is *ajam*, birthless, steady—like light and heat in the sun; therefore that knowledge which is *asaṁkrāntam*, unassociated with any other object; *ajam iṣyate*, is said to be unborn. *Yataḥ*, since; *jñānam*, the knowledge; *na kramate*, does not relate, to any other object; *tena*, because of that reason; it is *kīrtitam asaṅgam*, proclaimed to be non-relational like space.

अणुमात्रेऽपि वैधर्म्ये जायमानेऽविपश्चितः ।
असङ्गता सदा नास्ति किमुतावरणच्युतिः ॥९७॥

97. Should there occur any change for anything, however slight it may be, there can never be any non-attachment for the non-discriminating man;[1] what need one speak of the destruction of covering for him?

If, in accordance with the schools of disputants which differ from this, *jāyamāne vaidharmye aṇumātre api*, it be admitted that there is origination of any object of a different nature, inside or outside, however insignificant that origination be; then *na asti sadā*, there can never be; any *asaṅgatā*, non-attachment; *avipaścitaḥ*, for that non-discriminating man. *Kim uta*, what need one say that there is no; *āvaraṇacyutiḥ*, destruction of covering?

Objection: By asserting that there is no removal of covering, you lay yourself open to the charge of accept-

[1] For the slightest idea of origination carries with it the idea of the subject-object relation, i.e. duality.

ing a covering for the souls as your own conclusion.

To this it is *answered*, 'No'.

अलब्धावरणाः सर्वे धर्माः प्रकृतिनिर्मलाः ।
आदौ बुद्धास्तथा मुक्ता बुध्यन्त इति नायकाः ॥९८॥

98. No soul ever came under any veil. They are by nature pure as well as illumined and free from the very beginning. Thus being endowed with the power (of knowledge), they are said to know.

(*Sarve*) *dharmāḥ*, (all) the souls; *alabdhāvaraṇāḥ*, never had any veil, any bondage of ignorance etc., that is to say, they are free from bondage; and they are *prakṛtinirmalāḥ*, intrinsically pure; *buddhāḥ tathā muktāḥ*, illumined and also free; *ādau*, from the beginning, since they are by nature ever pure, illumined, and free. If they are so, why is it said that they *budhyante*, know? The answer is: They are *nāyakāḥ*, masters, have the power, of learning; that is to say, they are by nature endowed with the power of knowledge. This is just like saying, 'The sun shines', though the very nature of the sun is constant effulgence; or like saying, 'The hills stand', though it is the very nature of the hills to be perpetually motionless.

क्रमते न हि बुद्धस्य ज्ञानं धर्मेषु तायिनः ।
सर्वे धर्मास्तथा ज्ञानं नैतद्बुद्धेन भाषितम् ॥९९॥

99. The knowledge of the enlightened man, who is all-pervasive, does not extend to objects; all the

souls, also, like knowledge (do not reach out to objects). This view was not expressed by Buddha.

Hi, since; *jñānam*, the knowledge; *buddhasya*, of the enlightened one who has realized the ultimate Reality; *tāyinaḥ*, of the all-pervading one, of the one who has no interstices like space, or of the one who is either adorable or enlightened; *na kramate*, does not extend to; other *dharmeṣu*, objects; that is to say, his knowledge is ever centred in (or identified with) the soul, like light in the sun; *tathā*, similarly, like knowledge itself; *sarve dharmāḥ*, all the souls also; do not extend to other things whatsoever, the souls being analogous to (the all-pervasive) space. This is the meaning. The knowledge that was introduced in, 'through his knowledge that is comparable to space' (*Kārikā*, IV. 1), is this knowledge that is analogous to space, that does not reach out to other things, and that belongs to the enlightened one who is all-pervasive by virtue of his identity with knowledge itself. So also are the souls. Hence they are the reality that is the Self, Brahman, which like space is unchanging, immutable, partless, eternal, non-dual, unattached, invisible, unthinkable, beyond hunger etc., as is said in the Vedic text, 'for the vision of the witness can never be lost' (Bṛ. IV. iii. 23). That the nature of the supreme Reality is free from the differences of knowledge, known, and knower, and is without a second, *etat*, this fact; *na bhāṣitam*, was not expressed; *buddhena*, by Buddha; though a near approach to non-dualism was implied in his negation of outer objects and his imagination of everything as mere consciousness. But this non-duality, the essence of the ultimate Reality, is to be known from the Upaniṣads only. This is the purport.

At the end of the treatise a salutation is uttered in praise of the knowledge of the supreme Reality:

दुर्दर्शमतिगम्भीरमजं साम्यं विशारदम् ।
बुद्ध्वा पदमनानात्वं नमस्कुर्मो यथाबलम् ॥१००॥

100. After realizing that State of non-duality which is inscrutable, very profound, birthless, uniform, and holy, we make our obeisance to It to the best of our ability.

Durdarśam, that which can be seen with difficulty, that is to say, inscrutable, It being devoid of the four alternatives of existence, non-existence, etc. (*Kārikā*, IV. 83); and hence *atigambhīram*, very profound, unfathomable like an ocean — to the people lacking in discrimination. *Ajam*, birthless; *sāmyam*, uniform; *viśāradam*, holy. *Buddhvā*, having realized, having become identified with; such a *padam*, State; which is *anānātvam*, non-duality; *namaskurmaḥ*, we make our obeisance, to that State; *yathābalam*, to the best of our ability, by bringing It within the range of empirical dealings, though It defies all relative experience. This is the idea.

अजमपि जनियोगं प्रापदैश्वर्ययोगा-
दगति च गतिमन्यां प्रापदेकं ह्यनेकम् ।
विविधविषयधर्मग्राहिमुग्धेक्षणानां
प्रणतभयविहंतृ ब्रह्म यत्तन्नतोऽस्मि ॥१॥

प्रज्ञावैशाखवेधक्षुभितजलनिधेर्वेदनाम्नोऽन्तरस्थं
भूतान्यालोक्य मग्नान्यविरतजननग्राहघोरे समुद्रे।
कारुण्यादुद्दधारामृतमिदममरैर्दुर्लभं भूतहेतो-
र्यस्तं पूज्याभिपूज्यं परमगुरुममुं पादपातैर्नतोऽस्मि ॥२॥

यत्प्रज्ञालोकभासा प्रतिहतिमगमत्स्वान्तमोहांधकारो
मज्जोन्मज्जच्च घोरे ह्यसकृदुपजनोदन्वतित्रासने मे।
यत्पादावाश्रितानां श्रुतिशमविनयप्राप्तिरग्र्या ह्यमोघा
तत्पादौ पावनीयौ भवभयविनुदौ सर्वभावैर्नमस्ये ॥३॥

Salutation by the commentator:

1. I bow down to that Brahman which, though birthless, appears to be born through Its inscrutable power; which, though ever quiescent, appears to be in motion; which, though one, appears to be multiple to those whose vision has become perverted by the perception of diverse attributes of objects; and which destroys the fear of those who take shelter in It.

2. I salute by prostrating myself at the feet of that teacher of my teacher,[1] the most adorable among the adorable, who, on seeing the creatures drowned in the terrible sea (of the world) infested with sea-monsters in the form of repeated births, extricated, out of compassion for all beings, this nectar, which is difficult to be obtained even by gods and which lies in the depths of the ocean called the Vedas, which (Vedas)

[1] Gauḍapāda, the teacher of Govindapāda who taught Śaṅkara.

stirred up by inserting the churning rod of his illumined intellect.

3. I offer my obeisance with my whole being to those sanctifying feet—the dispellers of the fear of transmigration—(the feet) of my own teacher, through the light of whose illumined intellect was dispelled the darkness of delusion enveloping my own mind, who destroyed for ever my fear of appearance and disappearance in this terrible sea of innumerable births, and having taken shelter at whose feet others also get unfailingly the knowledge of the Upaniṣads, self-control, and humility, which is fruitful and most worthy.

INDEX TO THE TEXT OF MĀṆḌŪKYA UPANIṢAD

अमात्रश्चतुर्थो	...	12
ओमित्येतदक्षरमिदम्	...	1
एष सर्वेश्वर एष सर्वज्ञः	...	6
जागरितस्थानो बहि-	...	3
,, वैश्वानरः	...	9
नान्तःप्रज्ञं न बहिष्प्रज्ञम्	...	7
यत्र सुप्तो न कञ्चन कामम्	...	5
सर्वँ ह्येतद् ब्रह्मायमात्मा	...	2
सुषुप्तस्थानः प्राज्ञो	...	11
सोऽयमात्माऽध्यक्षरम्	...	8
स्वप्नस्थानस्तैजस	...	10
स्वप्नस्थानोऽन्तःप्रज्ञः	...	4

INDEX TO THE ŚLOKAS OF GAUḌAPĀDA'S KĀRIKĀ

अकल्पकमजं ज्ञानं	III.	33
अकारो नयते विश्वम्	I.	23
अजः कल्पितसंवृत्या	IV.	74
अजमनिद्रमस्वप्नम्	III.	36
,,	IV.	81
अजातस्यैव धर्मस्य	IV.	6
अजातस्यैव भावस्य	III.	20
अजातेस्त्रसतां तेषाम्	IV.	43
अजातं जायते यस्मात्	IV.	29
अजाद्वै जायते यस्य	IV.	13
अजेष्वजमसंक्रान्तं	IV.	96
अजे साम्ये तु ये	IV.	95
अणुमात्रेऽपि वैधर्म्ये	IV.	97
अतो वक्ष्याम्यकार्पण्यम्	III.	2
अदीर्घत्वाच्च कालस्य	II.	2
अद्वयं च द्वयाभासं	III.	30
,,	IV.	62
अद्वैतं परमार्थो हि	III.	18
अनादिमायया सुप्तः	I.	16
अनादेरन्तवत्त्वं च	IV.	30
अनिमित्तस्य चित्तस्य	IV.	77
अनिश्चिता यथा रज्जुः	II.	7
अन्तःस्थानात्तु भेदानां	II.	4
अन्यथा गृह्णतः स्वप्नः	I.	15
अपूर्वं स्थानिधर्मो हि	II.	8
अभावश्च रथादीनां	II.	3
अभूताभिनिवेशाद्धि	IV.	79
अभूताभिनिवेशोऽस्ति	IV.	75
अमात्रोऽनन्तमात्रश्च	I.	29
अलब्धावरणाः सर्वे	IV.	98
अलाते स्पन्दमाने वै	IV.	49
अवस्त्वनुपलम्भं च	IV.	88
अव्यक्ता एव येऽन्तस्तु	II.	15
अशक्तिरपरिज्ञानं	IV.	19
असज्जागरिते दृष्ट्वा	IV.	39
असतो मायया जन्म	III.	28
अस्ति नास्त्यस्ति	IV.	83
अस्पन्दमानमलातं	IV.	48
अस्पर्शयोगो वै नाम	III.	39
,,	IV.	2
आत्मसत्यानुबोधेन	III.	32
आत्मा ह्याकाशवत्	III.	3
आदावन्ते च यन्नास्ति	II.	6
,,	IV.	31
आदिबुद्धाः प्रकृत्यैव	IV.	92
आदिशान्ता ह्यनुत्पन्नाः	IV.	93

आश्रमास्त्रिविधा III. 16
इच्छामात्रं प्रभोः सृष्टिः I. 8
उत्पादस्याप्रसिद्धत्वात् IV. 38
उत्सेक उदधेर्यद्वत् III. 41
उपलम्भात् समाचारात् IV. 42
" IV. 44
उपायेन निगृह्णीयात् III. 42
उपासनाश्रितो धर्मो III. 1
उभयोरपि वैतथ्यं II. 11
उभे ह्यन्योन्यदृश्ये ते IV. 67
ऋजुवक्रादिकाभासम् IV. 47
एतैरेषोऽपृथग्भावैः II. 30
एवं न चित्तजा धर्माः IV. 54
एवं न जायते चित्तम् IV. 46
ओंकारं पादशो विद्यात् I. 24
कल्पयत्यात्मनाऽऽत्मानम् II. 12
कार्यकारणबद्धौ ताविष्येते I. 11
कारणाद्यद्यनन्यत्वं IV. 12
कारणं यस्य वै कार्यं IV. 11
काल इति कालविदः II. 24
कोटयश्चतस्र एतास्तु IV. 84
क्रमते न हि बुद्धस्य IV. 99
ख्याप्यमानामजातिं IV. 5
ग्रहणाज्जागरितवत् IV. 37
ग्रहो न तत्र नोत्सर्गः III. 38
घटादिषु प्रलीनेषु III. 4
चरञ्जागरिते जाग्रत् IV. 65
चित्तकाला हि ये II. 14
चित्तं न संस्पृशत्यर्थं IV. 26
चित्तस्पन्दितमेवेदं IV. 72
जरामरणनिर्मुक्ताः IV. 10
जाग्रच्चित्तेक्षणीयास्ते IV. 66
जाग्रद्वृत्तावपि त्वन्तः II. 10
जात्याभासं चलाभासं IV. 45
जीवात्मनोः पृथक्त्वं यत् III. 14
जीवात्मनोरनन्यत्वम् III. 13
जीवं कल्पयते पूर्वं II. 16
ज्ञाने च त्रिविधे ज्ञेये IV. 89
ज्ञानेनाकाशकल्पेन IV. 1
तत्त्वमाध्यात्मिकं दृष्ट्वा II. 38
तस्मादेवं विदित्वैनं II. 36
तस्मान्न जायते चित्तं IV. 28
तैजसस्योत्वविज्ञान I. 20
त्रिषु धामसु यस्तुल्यं I. 22
त्रिषु धामसु यद्भोज्यं I. 5
दक्षिणाक्षिमुखे विश्वः I. 2
दुःखं सर्वमनुस्मृत्य III. 43
दुर्दर्शमतिगम्भीरं IV. 100
द्रव्यं द्रव्यस्य हेतुः IV. 53
द्वयोर्द्वयोर्मधुज्ञाने III. 12
द्वैतस्याग्रहणं तुल्यं I. 13
धर्मा य इति जायन्ते IV. 58
न कश्चिज्जायते जीवः III. 48
" IV. 71
न निरोधो न चोत्पत्तिः II. 32
न निर्गता अलातात्ते IV. 50

न निर्गतास्ते विज्ञानात्	IV.	52
न भवत्यमृतं मर्त्यम्	III.	21
,,	IV.	7
न युक्तं दर्शनं गत्वा	IV.	34
नाकाशस्य घटाकाशो	III.	7
नाजेषु सर्वधर्मेषु	IV.	60
नात्मभावेन नानेदं	II.	34
नात्मानं न परां	I.	12
नास्त्यसद्धेतुकमसत्	IV.	40
नास्वादयेत्सुखं तत्र	III.	45
निगृहीतस्य मनसः	III.	34
निमित्तं न सदा चित्तं	IV.	27
निवृत्तस्याप्रवृत्तस्य	IV.	80
निवृत्तेः सर्वदुःखानाम्	I.	10
निश्चितायां यथा रज्ज्वां	II.	18
निस्तुतिर्निर्नमस्कारः	II.	37
नेह नानेति चाम्नायात्	III.	24
पञ्चविंशक इत्येके	II.	26
पादा इति पादविदः	II.	21
पूर्वापरापरिज्ञानं	IV.	21
प्रकृत्याऽऽकाशवज्ज्ञेयाः	IV.	91
प्रज्ञप्तेः सनिमित्तत्वं	IV.	24
,,	IV.	25
प्रणवं हीश्वरं विद्यात्	I.	28
प्रणवो ह्यपरं ब्रह्म	I.	26
प्रपञ्चो यदि विद्येत	I.	17
प्रभवः सर्वभावानां	I.	6
प्राण इति प्राणविदः	II.	20
प्राणादिभिरनन्तैश्च	II.	19
प्राप्य सर्वज्ञतां कृत्स्नां	IV.	85
फलादुत्पद्यमानः सन्	IV.	17
बहिष्प्रज्ञो विभुर्विश्वः	I.	1
बीजाङ्कुराख्यो दृष्टान्तः	IV.	20
बुद्ध्वाऽनिमित्ततां सत्यां	IV.	78
भावैरसद्भिरेवायं	II.	33
भूततोऽभूततो वाऽपि	III.	23
भूतस्य जातिमिच्छन्ति	IV.	3
भूतं न जायते किंचित्	IV.	4
भोगार्थं सृष्टिरित्यन्ये	I.	9
मकारभावे प्राज्ञस्य	I.	21
मन इति मनोविदः	II.	25
मनसो निग्रहायत्तं	III.	40
मनोदृश्यमिदं द्वैतं	III.	31
मरणे संभवे चैव	III.	9
मायया भिद्यते ह्येतत्	III.	19
मित्राद्यैः सह संमन्त्र्य	IV.	35
मृल्लोहविस्फुलिङ्गाद्यैः	III.	15
यथा निर्मितको जीवः	IV.	70
यथा भवति बालानां	III.	8
यथा मायामयाद् बीजात्	IV.	59
यथा मायामयो जीवः	IV.	69
यथा स्वप्नमयो जीवः	IV.	68
यथा स्वप्ने द्वयाभासं	III.	29
,,	IV.	61
यथैकस्मिन् घटाकाशे	III.	5
यदा न लभते हेतून्	IV.	76

यदा न लीयते चित्तं	III.	46
यदि हेतोः फलात् सिद्धिः	IV.	18
यावद्धेतुफलावेशः	IV.	55
,,	IV.	56
युञ्जीत प्रणवे चेतः	I.	25
योऽस्ति कल्पितसंवृत्या	IV.	73
यं भावं दर्शयेद्यस्य	II.	29
रसादयो हि ये कोशा	III.	11
रूपकार्यसमाख्याश्च	III.	6
लये संबोधयेच्चित्तं	III.	44
लीयते ही सुषुप्ते तत्	III.	35
लोकाँल्लोकविदः प्राहुः	II.	27
विकरोत्यपरान् भावान्	II.	13
विकल्पो विनिवर्तेत	I.	18
विज्ञाने स्पन्दमाने वै	IV.	51
विपर्यासाद्यथा जाग्रत्	IV.	41
विप्राणां विनयो ह्येष	IV.	86
विभूतिं प्रसवं त्वन्ये	I.	7
विश्वस्यात्वविवक्षायां	I.	19
विश्वो हि स्थूलभुङ्नित्यं	I.	3
वीतरागभयक्रोधैः	II.	35
वेदा इति वेदविदः	II.	22
वैतथ्यं सर्वभावानां	II.	1
वैशारद्यं तु वै नास्ति	IV.	94
स एष नेति नेतीति	III.	26
सतो हि मायया जन्म	III.	27
सप्रयोजनता तेषां	II.	7
,,	IV.	32
संघाताः स्वप्नवत्सर्वे	III.	10
संभवे हेतुफलयोः	IV.	16
संभूतेरपवादाच्च	III.	25
संवृत्या जायते सर्वं	IV.	57
सर्वस्य प्रणवो ह्यादिः	I.	27
सर्वाभिलापविगतः	III.	37
सर्वे धर्मा मृषा स्वप्ने	IV.	33
सवस्तु सोपलम्भं च	IV.	87
सांसिद्धिकी स्वाभाविकी	IV.	9
सुखमाव्रियते नित्यं	IV.	82
सूक्ष्म इति सूक्ष्मविदः	II.	23
सृष्टिरिति सृष्टिविदः	II.	28
स्थूलं तर्पयते विश्वं	I.	4
स्वतो वा परतो वाऽपि	IV.	22
स्वप्नजागरितस्थाने	II.	5
स्वप्नदृक्चित्तदृश्यास्ते	IV.	64
स्वप्नदृक् प्रचरन् स्वप्ने	IV.	63
स्वप्ननिद्रायुतावाद्यौ	I.	14
स्वप्नमाये यथा दृष्टे	II.	31
स्वप्नवृत्तावपि त्वन्तः	II.	9
स्वप्ने चावस्तुकः कायः	IV.	36
स्वभावेनामृतो यस्य	III.	22
,,	IV.	8
स्वसिद्धान्तव्यवस्थासु	III.	17
स्वस्थं शान्तं सनिर्वाणं	III.	47
हेतुर्न जायतेऽनादेः	IV.	23
हेतोरादिः फलं येषां	IV.	14
,,	IV.	15
हेयज्ञेयाप्यपाक्यानि	IV.	90